PEACE, WAR AND NEUTRALITY

BRITAIN
NORTHERN IRELAND
AND ÉIRE
1935-1949

NORMAN JOHNSTON

SHEILA JOHNSTON

Colourpoint

The author would like to give special thanks to the following people: Richard Collins for access to his advice and resources; Richard Neil for information on Castle Archdale; and Wesley and Kathleen Twist who gave of their time and memories so generously.

8 7 6 5 4 3

© Norman Johnston
Newtownards
1997

ISBN (Foundation level) 1 898392 31 5

Layout and design: Colourpoint Books
Printed by: W & G Baird Ltd

COLOURPOINT BOOKS
Unit D5, Ards Business Centre
Jubilee Road
NEWTOWNARDS
Co Down
BT23 4YH

Tel: (028) 9182 0505
Fax: (028) 9182 1900
E-mail: info@colourpoint.co.uk
Web-site: www.colourpoint.co.uk

J171,508
€ 9.00

A note from the author on terminology

The period of history covered by this book is a minefield for those who must use names such as Ireland, Éire, Free State, etc. Probably unsuccessfully, I have endeavoured to annoy no-one, and to strive merely for consistency. The Irish form of Ireland — Éire — has been used throughout for the Irish Free State after 1937. This is to avoid confusion with those parts of the text where the word 'Ireland' means the whole island, including Northern Ireland. Contemporary sources used in the book refer to Éire also.
Problems also arise when naming Derry/Londonderry. In this case I hope I have been liberal and random in the use of both. I hope readers will, at least, be tolerant of my difficulty!
Norman Johnston

Acknowledgements:
© AFF/AFS Amsterdam: 48B
Agusti Centelles, Barcelona: 16A
Author's collection: 39F, 42A, 51C, 53D, 53E, 55C
Belfast Telegraph: 33A, 41D, 43D, 48A
HC Casserly: 57B
R Collins collection: 14A, 14B
Colour-Rail: 56A
Leo Coyle: 35C
Daily Mail: 22A, 30A, 39E, 50A
Dublin Opinion: 61B
By kind permission of Mr Rowel Friers: 11C
Home Front Heritage Centre: 31C, 32E
Hulton Getty: 6A, 7B, 7C, 9B, 9C, 11B, 25A, 50B
Imperial War Museum: 29C, 33B, 33C, 33D, 35B, 35D, 35G, 38A, 38B, 38C, 38D, 40B
Norman Johnston: 4, 20A, 25C, 26A, 28E, rear cover
Sheila Johnston: 8A, 40A
Keystone Collection: 23D
Robert McKergan: 35F
Ian Mullen: 35E
PRONI: 41C
WE Robertson: Cover upper, 10A, 52A, 54A, 55B
Time-Life Colorific!: 15C, 21C, 27B, 27C
W Twist: 43C
Ulster Aviation Society: 36A, 36B, 44A
Voice of Ulster: 60A

Norman Johnston is a retired History teacher. He was Head of History at Omagh Academy, Co Tyrone, from 1980 to 1996 and was Moderator for GCSE History Coursework in N. Ireland from 1991 to 1997. He is now a full time publisher and writer. He is author of *The Norman Impact on the Medieval World* and co-author of *Britain Ireland and Europe from 1570-1745*, both published by Colourpoint. He is now preparing a GCSE textbook on Weimar and Nazi Germany.

Sheila Johnston is a graduate of Queen's University, Belfast. She was College Librarian in Fermanagh College, then manager of the Study Centre in Omagh College, Co Tyrone, until 1994. She has published many short stories and articles as well as contributing to local radio. She has written a biography, and co-produced a documentary for Radio Ulster, on Alice Milligan and edited a book of her poems. She is now a full time publisher and writer .

CONTENTS

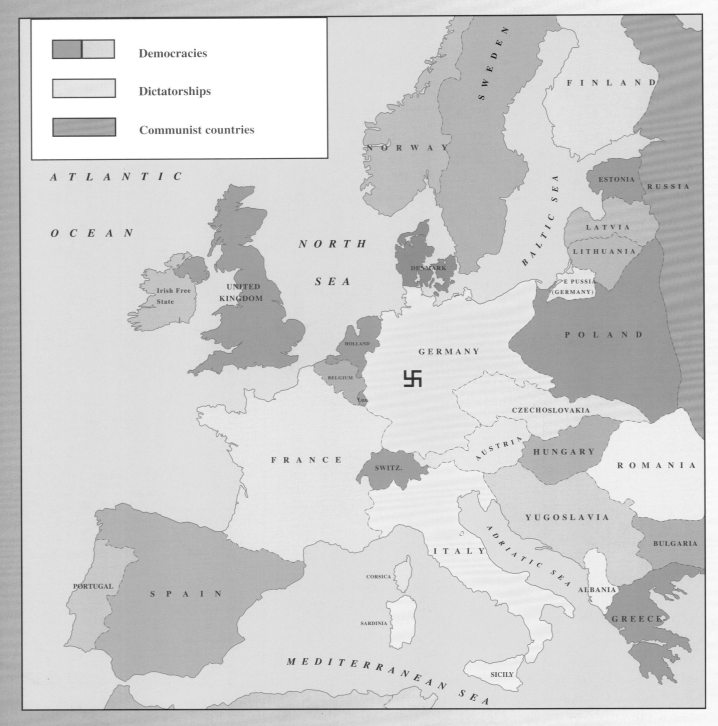

Democracies

Dictatorships

Communist countries

In 1935 Britain and Germany were at peace. They had even signed a Naval Agreement. This made Hitler, the leader of Germany, very pleased.

Five years later Britain and Germany were enemies. The Second World War had begun in 1939.

This book will explain how this happened. It will also tell you about life in Northern Ireland and the Irish Free State during the war.

- Northern Ireland was part of the United Kingdom and was involved in the war.

- The Irish Free State was neutral and did not take part in the war.

THE COUNTRIES OF EUROPE IN 1935

In 1935 there were three different sorts of country in Europe:

1 Democracies
2 Dictatorships
3 Communist countries

By looking at the map you can see all these countries. The colours will tell you what sort they were.

1 Democracies

Most countries in Europe were democracies, including the United Kingdom and the Irish Free State. In a democracy there was a parliament, elected by the people who lived in the country. This gave the people who lived in the country a say in how the country was governed. In a democracy people had freedom and they had rights.

Some countries had not been democracies for very long. At the end of the First World War (1914-1918) some countries became independent for the first time. Examples are Poland and Czechoslovakia.

2 Dictatorships

Germany and Italy were not democracies. They were dictatorships. In a dictatorship there was no proper parliament The people had no say in how the country was governed, because there were no elections. Instead there was a dictator who told everyone what to do. **Hitler** was dictator of Germany and **Mussolini** was dictator of Italy. In a dictatorship people did not have much freedom or many rights. If they criticised the government they were put in jail. The dictators were helped by their followers. Hitler's followers were called Nazis and Mussolini's followers were called Fascists. These followers had special privileges and were given a lot of power.

3 Communist countries

The only communist country in 1935 was Russia. In 1917 there had been a revolution there. The Tsar or Emperor of Russia was overthrown and the communists took control of the country. They tried to make everyone equal. No one was allowed to own more than anyone else. The government took over all the factories and farms. People could not work for themselves. Everyone was employed by the government.

A lot of people did not like this, but the communists imprisoned anyone who disagreed. In this way they were a bit like the dictators. The leader of Russia was a communist called **Stalin**.

Stalin wanted other countries to become communist. He had an organisation called the Communist International which tried to encourage revolutions in places like Britain, France and Germany. Other countries did not like Russia and were afraid of communists.

?

1 Look at the map and name five countries that were democracies in 1935.

2 Write 'Democracy' on one side of a page and 'Dictatorship' on the other side. Now list the differences between them.

5

1.2 BRITAIN IN 1935

We can get an idea of what Britain was like in 1935 by looking at five topics.

1 The Economy

The Industrial Revolution in the 19th century made some industries very important to Britain. These were industries like coal-mining, ship-building and iron and steel production. After the First World War (1914 - 1918) countries all over the world found that they had less money to

A busy street in Cambridge, England, in 1935.

spend trading with each other. So at the beginning of the 20th century Britain found that it was exporting fewer goods. In particular, the ship-building industry was not doing well, because fewer ships were needed.

Many people were out of work for a long time. In 1932 there were 2.7 million people unemployed in Britain. In Germany, 5.6 million were unemployed. While it is not good to be unemployed at any time, it was particularly hard in the 1930s. People were paid a lot less. A man's pay packet couldn't buy as much then as the pay packet of a man doing the same job today. Also, people then couldn't get so much money on the dole or from other government allowances. Nowadays, there are sometimes two people in a family working. In the 1930s, usually only one person in a family had a job, so if that job was lost, then the family was really poor.

2 Social life

If you *did* have a job, the 1930s were a good time. Prices went down, so people with money had more to spend. Factories produced more ready-made clothes and more people could buy things like furniture, radios and gramophones. (Gramophones played music like our tapes and CDs today.)

Families were able to get about more because of better public transport. There were buses and many larger towns and cities had trams. The fares were cheap. Bicycles were very popular.

There were a lot more railways then than there are now. Special trains ran to give even the poorest people a trip to the seaside.

There were some cars, but only the better off people could afford one. An Austin Seven cost £100 and most people earned less than £4 a week.

New council houses were built for the poorest people who had been living in slums.

3 The Mass media

Newspapers could now print pictures as well as words and they were very cheap, so everyone could buy one.

Remember that there was no TV in the 1930s, although many households had radios. Millions of people went to the cinema every week. A film called *The Jazz Singer* was the first film to have a sound track. Before this films had been silent. Now films were called 'talkies'!

Cinemas also showed newsreels, and so it was in the cinema that people saw Hitler and Roosevelt for the first time.

Traffic in Hyde Park Corner, London, during the Silver Jubilee, 1935.

4 Politics

Stanley Baldwin became Prime Minister in 1935. He was a Conservative. He retired in 1937 and **Neville Chamberlain** became Prime Minister. The leader of the Labour Party was **Clement Attlee**. **Winston Churchill** said Attlee was " a modest little man with plenty to be modest about."

5 The Abdication crisis 1936

Edward VIII became king in 1936. He fell in love with an American woman called Mrs Simpson. She was divorced and the king wanted to marry her. She was very unpopular and there was a big row in the country. The king would not give up Mrs Simpson so he gave up the throne instead. His brother became King George VI and he was the father of Elizabeth II. 'To abdicate' means 'to give up'.

Stanley Baldwin, Prime Minister 1935-37.

?

1 Why were so many people out of work in the 1930s in Britain and why did this mean that families were very poor?

2 Look at Sources A and B. What would you expect to see if you visited these places today?

3 Use your school library to find out more about Stanley Baldwin, Neville Chamberlain and Clement Attlee.

In 1935, Ireland had been divided for only fourteen years. Up to 1921 all of Ireland had been part of the UK, but now it was divided into two parts:

1 The **Irish Free State** which was independent, and

2 **Northern Ireland** which was still part of the UK.

The Irish Free State

This had 26 counties. It was set up in 1922. It had its own parliament (called the **Dáil**) in Dublin, its own government, its own flag and its own army. But it was not completely independent of Britain because of the **Anglo-Irish Treaty** which was made in 1921.

All members of the Dáil and Irish government had to swear to be loyal to the King of England. They also had to accept that Northern Ireland would not be included in the Free State unless the Belfast government agreed.

A **Boundary Commission** was set up to decide exactly where the border would be.

Britain also insisted on keeping three ports in the Irish Free State so that it could keep Royal Navy ships there. This was in case there was another war with Germany. If Britain had ships based in the Free State, they could get to the Atlantic more quickly These three ports were called the **Treaty Ports**. It would be hard for the Free State not to take sides in a war that Britain was involved in, if there were British warships in its territory.

The Irish Government

Most people in the South were happy to see the Free State set up, but not *everyone* agreed. Some people, like **Éamon de Valera**, said the Free State was not independent enough and did not want Ireland to be divided. He wanted a **republic**.

A

Lough Swilly

LONDONDERRY

Donegal

Londonderry

Antrim

Tyrone

BELFAST

Leitrim

Fermanagh

Armagh

Down

Sligo

Monaghan

Mayo

Cavan

Louth

Roscommon

Longford

Meath

Galway

Westmeath

Dublin

GALWAY

Offaly

DUBLIN

Kildare

Laois

Wicklow

Clare

LIMERICK

Carlow

Limerick

Kilkenny

Wexford

Tipperary

Kerry

Waterford

Cork

CORK

Spike Island

Berehaven

	Northern Ireland
	Irish Free State
□	Treaty Ports

So, as soon as the Free State was set up, there was a **Civil War** between the two sides. This took place between 1922 and 1923. The Free State side won, but this war left many people with very bitter memories. Indeed, some people have not forgotten about it yet.

De Valera went on to form the **Fianna Fáil** party.

WT Cosgrave led the Irish Free State until 1932. He formed the party which is now called **Fine Gael**. In 1932 de Valera, the leader of Fianna Fáil became leader of the Irish Free State. Both these parties still exist today.

De Valera had always wanted a republic. Now he was leader he could do something about it.

B

W T Cosgrave, head of the Executive Council of the Irish Free State, 1922-32.

In 1933 he said no-one had to swear loyalty to the King of England any more. He also stopped paying some taxes to Britain. Britain hit back by putting high taxes on all goods that the Free State wanted to sell to Britain. So there was a **trade war** going on.

The Economy

The population of the Irish Free State was about 3 million. Even though it had some independence it was still affected very much by Britain. British coins were still used, even after the Free State started making its own coins in 1928.

The Free State still bought a lot of goods from Britain and it also sold most of its farm produce to Britain.

The Free State imported most of its sugar, so de Valera tried to get farmers to grow sugar beet so that the country could make its own sugar.

C

Éamon de Valera, head of the Executive Council of the Irish Free State, 1932-37 and Taoiseach, 1937-48.

?

1　In your own words, explain why Britain wanted to hold on to three naval ports in the Irish Free State.

2　Were Britain and the Irish Free State friendly towards each other in 1935? Explain your answer.

3　Sugar can be made from sugar beet. What is sugar beet?

9

An early view of the Northern Ireland Parliament building at Stormont. Note the trolley bus lines, long since disappeared.

In the six north-eastern counties of Ireland there were Unionists who did not want to be ruled by a government in Dublin.

So Northern Ireland was set up in **1921** by the **Government of Ireland Act (1920)**.

Northern Ireland stayed as part of the United Kingdom. It was protected by the British Army, flew the Union Jack, and used British stamps and coins. It also sent 12 MPs to the British parliament at Westminster.

Government

But Northern Ireland was still a bit different from the rest of the United Kingdom. You couldn't vote Labour or Conservative because these political parties organise there.

The main difference was that Northern Ireland was given its own parliament. In **1932**, a brand new parliament building, called **Stormont**, was opened near Belfast. People could elect 52 MPs to this local parliament. Most of the MPs in Stormont were Unionists. **Lord Craigavon** was Prime Minister from 1921 to 1940.

There were about $1\frac{1}{2}$ million people in Northern Ireland. Two thirds were Unionists and one third were Nationalists. The Nationalists didn't want to be part of Northern Ireland and were against the Unionist government. At first Nationalist MPs did not attend the Stormont parliament. Then, in 1925, the **Nationalist Party** decided it *would* go to the Stormont parliament as the official opposition party, in order to be able to speak for the Nationalist people. **Joseph Devlin** was their leader.

The IRA

The IRA was very much against the setting up of Northern Ireland. It wanted Ireland to stay united. In 1921 and 1922 the IRA carried out a lot of attacks. The Ulster Special Constabulary (B-Specials) were set up to fight IRA violence. Unfortunately, ordinary members of the Nationalist community were sometimes attacked and rioting and gun attacks were very common.

To try to get control, the Unionists passed the **Special Powers Act** in **1922**. This gave police the right to search any houses they wanted and to put people in jail without having to give them a trial first. The Special Powers Act was still law until 1971.

By 1923, the two sides had mostly stopped fighting, but still didn't trust each other. Because Unionists thought that Nationalists wanted to get rid of Northern Ireland they sometimes didn't help them with jobs or houses.

B

Lord Craigavon, Prime Minister of Northern Ireland 1921-40.

Nationalists didn't like being ruled by Unionists, and being cut off from the rest of Nationalist Ireland.

Nationalists and Unionists lived separate lives. They went to different schools and even had different clubs for sport.

By 1935, these differences didn't matter very much in everyday life. Farmers bought and sold animals at the same markets, business people traded with each other and people shopped in each others shops.

Even so, the Unionist people did seem to have more of the better farms, houses and jobs. But some people say that the setting up of Northern Ireland had not been the reason for this. This was the way it was long before Northern Ireland was set up.

C

"On the other hand, it's quite possible his story of taking a wrong turning could be perfectly true."

The border between Northern Ireland and the Free State offered temptations to smugglers.

SOURCE

?

1 Write a note about how Northern Ireland was governed in 1935.

2 Do you think the cartoon (Source C) supports (a) the Nationalist point of view , (b) the Unionist point of view, or (c) neither?

3 While the two communities were very divided, can you see, in this unit, any ways in which ordinary people got on quite well together?

B-Specials search a cart at a border crossing. Does this scene look posed?

The Irish Free State and Northern Ireland

At this time the two parts of Ireland were not very friendly towards each other. De Valera still wanted to do away with the border. This made the northern Unionists very wary of having anything to do with the South.

The Anglo-Irish Trade War

You read about this first on page 9. The taxes which the Free State stopped paying to Britain were to do with land and were paid by farmers. Farmers paid nearly 5 million pounds a year to Britain. When de Valera ordered that farmers should stop paying these taxes, Britain was annoyed. It taxed all Free State goods which were sold in the United Kingdom. This was good for items from Northern Ireland, because Northern Ireland was in the UK and its goods were not taxed.

Then de Valera put a tax on all goods coming *into* the Free State from the UK. This *did* include goods from Northern Ireland being sold to the South. This affected trade with Britain and Northern Ireland quite badly.

The 1937 Free State Constitution

De Valera was still trying to get rid of as much of the Anglo-Irish Treaty as he could. You learned in chapter 1.3 that he said that people did not have to swear loyalty to the King of England any more. He did more things like this to try to cut the Free State off more and more from any influence by Britain. He made the most of the abdication crisis (which you read about in chapter 1.2), saying that the king had shown that he wasn't very important at all.

By **1937**, so many things had changed since the Anglo-Irish Treaty of 1921, that it

B

2 THE NATIONAL TERRITORY CONSISTS OF THE WHOLE ISLAND OF IRELAND, ITS ISLANDS AND THE TERRITORIAL SEAS.

3 PENDING THE RE-INTEGRATION OF THE NATIONAL TERRITORY, AND WITHOUT PREJUDICE TO THE RIGHT OF THE PARLIAMENT AND GOVERNMENT ESTABLISHED BY THIS CONSTITUTION TO EXERCISE JURISDICTION OVER THE WHOLE OF THAT TERRITORY, THE LAWS ENACTED BY THAT PARLIAMENT SHALL HAVE THE LIKE AREA AND EXTENT OF APPLICATION AS THE LAWS OF SAORSTÁT ÉIREANN AND THE LIKE EXTRA-TERRITORIAL EFFECT.

4 THE NAME OF THE STATE IS ÉIRE, OR IN THE ENGLISH LANGUAGE, **IRELAND**.

7 THE NATIONAL FLAG IS THE TRICOLOUR OF GREEN, WHITE AND ORANGE.

8.1 THE IRISH LANGUAGE AS THE NATIONAL LANGUAGE IS THE FIRST OFFICIAL LANGUAGE.

8.2 THE ENGLISH LANGUAGE IS RECOGNISED AS A SECOND OFFICIAL LANGUAGE.

ARTICLE 44

1.2° THE STATE RECOGNISES THE SPECIAL POSITION OF THE HOLY CATHOLIC APOSTOLIC AND ROMAN CHURCH AS THE GUARDIAN OF THE FAITH PROFESSED BY THE GREAT MAJORITY OF THE CITIZENS.

1.3° THE STATE ALSO RECOGNISES THE CHURCH OF IRELAND, THE PRESBYTERIAN CHURCH IN IRELAND, THE METHODIST CHURCH IN IRELAND, THE RELIGIOUS SOCIETY OF FRIENDS IN IRELAND, AS WELL AS THE JEWISH CONGREGATIONS AND THE OTHER RELIGIOUS DENOMINATIONS EXISTING IN IRELAND AT THE DATE OF THE COMING INTO OPERATION OF THIS CONSTITUTION.

SOURCE *Extracts from the 1937* **Constitution of Ireland**.

?

1 If you were a northern Nationalist, what would you think of Articles 2, 3, 4, 7 and 8 of the Irish Constitution?

2 There is an important difference between the two parts of Article 44 (1.2° and 1.3°). What do think it is?

seemed a good idea to make a whole new set of rules about the way the Free State was governed. In fact, a new Irish Constitution was set up. The 1937 constitution is the one which is still followed today.

The main changes in the new constitution were:

1 The King of England was not the Head of State any more. Now there was a **President**.

2 The leader of the government was to be known as the **Taoiseach**, which is the Irish word for Prime Minister.

3 The new constitution said that Northern Ireland should not exist and that the South of Ireland had a right to rule it. (See Source B).

4 The Free State said that the Roman Catholic Church had a very special place in the country, but it did also say that anyone could belong to any religion they wanted.

This meant that the Free State was acting like a republic, even if no one had actually made it one yet. Unionists in Northern Ireland were alarmed at the claim that the South had a right to rule it.

Top: Adolph Hitler.

Right: Nazi rally at Nuremburg in 1933.

By the middle of the 1930s, there were more and more signs that there might be a war on the continent. This worried Britain. The dictators were now very strong, and the rest of the European countries, especially Britain and France, were not really sure what to do about this.

They had four reasons in mind for not going to war:

1   The Dread of War
The First World War was supposed to have been 'the war to end all wars'. It had been such a bad experience that countries really did not want to have another war.

2   Money matters
The First World War had cost countries a lot of money and had left them with huge war debts. You read on page 6 about how countries like England and France were not doing very well in the 1930s and many people were poor and unemployed. It takes a lot of money to run an army. Going to war again just didn't seem like a good idea.

3   What people thought
Most of the general public was against war. Most families in Britain and France had lost fathers, sons and brothers in the First World War, and no one wanted to go through that again. So if a government wanted peace and not war it was much more likely to be elected.

4   Sympathy with Germany
When countries were making peace after the First World War, Germany was not allowed to have as big an army as other countries in Europe, and it was not allowed to have any troops in part of Germany called the Rhineland. In Britain, some people felt this *had* been a little unfair on Germany and maybe Hitler had a good point.

The Dictators 1933-1936

1933 Hitler comes to power in Germany and begins to rearm.
Germany leaves the League of Nations.

1934 Hitler signs a Non-aggression Pact with Poland.
Austrian Nazis murder their Prime Minister. Mussolini intervenes to prevent a Nazi takeover.

1935 Saar votes to rejoin Germany.
Hitler introduces conscription and announces the existance of the Luftwaffe.
Britain, France and Italy agree to co-operate against Hitler (Stresa Front).
Britain signs the Anglo-German Naval Agreement.
Mussolini invades Ethiopia.

1936 Hitler remilitarises the Rhineland.
Mussolini completes his conquest of Abyssinia.
Spanish Civil War begins.
Rome-Berlin Axis created.

?

1 Read the reasons opposite for *not* going to war. Can you think of reasons why Britain *should* go to war?

2 Think of all you have learnt so far about the situation in Europe in the 1930s. If you were Prime Minister of Britain then, what would *you* have done?

C *Benito Mussolini*

Reaction to Hitler

So the democratic countries in Europe decided to ignore the fact that Germany was building up weapons again. The French were very alarmed by Hitler, but they would not do anything against him without Britain's support.

Mussolini — friend or foe?

In the First World War, Italy had been on Britain's side. France and Britain tried to cooperate with Mussolini. But then Mussolini invaded Ethiopia in 1935. France and Britain tried to avoid a row about this but in the end they had to join with other countries in punishing Italy by stopping trade in some goods. Germany was not involved so Hitler got Mussolini onto his side, and in 1936 these two dictators signed an agreement with each other, called the **Rome-Berlin Axis**.

In 1936 the democracies in Europe were not very happy with what was happening. Two dictators, Hitler and Mussolini, were now working together and had shown that they did not really care what other countries thought of what they did.

The Spanish Civil War 1936-1939

Up to this time, Spain had been a democracy, but in 1936 a general in the Spanish army, called **Franco**, led a revolt against the democratically elected government. Franco was a **fascist**.

This caused a civil war which lasted for three years. A million people were killed.

Germany and Italy were on Franco's side. They helped by giving Franco weapons. They also used

Street fighting in Barcelona during the Spanish Civil War.

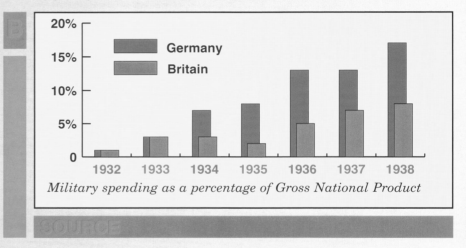

Military spending as a percentage of Gross National Product

the war to test out some of their own tanks and aircraft. Germany supplied planes and pilots which were called the Condor Legion.

People in the rest of Europe were very unhappy about Franco's revolt. Countries would not go to fight Franco, but many individual people went over to Spain to fight against fascism. They joined the **International Brigades**. Some Ulster Protestants were among those to go.

Some people volunteered to fight *for* Franco also. There were the **Blueshirts** from the Irish Free State and the **Blackshirts** from England.

Rearmament

So what were the democracies to do about this rise of fascism and dictatorship?

Countries like Belgium just hoped that nobody would bother with them because they were too small. The countries with the best armies were Britain, France, Czechoslovakia and Poland.

Germany had a very modern army, because it had been building it up since 1934. They had all the latest weapons and made the armies of other countries look very old fashioned. They had a specially good airforce, called the **Luftwaffe**.

BRITAIN'S OPTIONS FOR DEALING WITH THE DICTATORS

1 Stand up to the dictators by threatening war if they make any more moves. Begin rearming to catch up on Germany, so that if war comes Britain will not be defeated.

2 Don't rearm. Rely on negotiations and the League of Nations to deal with any demands or threat that the dictators might make. Rearming will only make the dictators more aggressive.

3 Buy time, by making concessions to the dictators, so that Britain has time to rearm and be ready, should the worst come to the worst and war ensue.

Neutrality

Neutrality means not taking anyone's side. Britain couldn't be neutral against Hitler. He was too much of a threat. He wanted Germany to take over Europe and Britain was getting in his way.

But the Irish Free State *could* be neutral. Here are the reasons why:

1 Ireland was fairly small and poor. Germany probably would not want to invade it. An invasion would have to be by sea, and it would not be worth the effort.
2 The Free State didn't want to be a big power anyway. If they stayed neutral they wouldn't have to spend a lot of money on an army.
3 The Irish Free State knew that Britain could not risk allowing the Germans to take over Ireland.
4 The Free State could show that it was now independent by showing that Britain's enemies did not have to be Ireland's enemies as well.
5 In the First World War, Irish Nationalists had tried to get German support against England, and had used German guns in the Easter Rising. So some of the people who ruled the Free State now had more sympathy with Germany than with Britain.

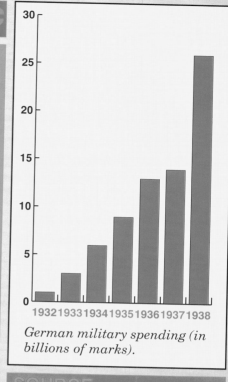

C

German military spending (in billions of marks).

SOURCE

?

1 Why would anyone from England want to fight *for* Franco?

2 Look at the graph in Source B. Using this as evidence, what year did Germany start to build up its armed forces? What did Britain do with its armed forces the next year?

3 Study the arguments in favour of Irish neutrality. Which ones do you think are most important?

17

1.8 Anglo-Irish relations, 1937-38

Britain's rearmament

Because of the power the dictators had now in Europe, Britain felt it should build up its armed forces again. In 1935, important decisions were made. These were:

1 To make the Royal Navy a lot bigger.
2 To make the RAF three times bigger.
3 To build a new fighter aeroplane which could fight the Germans if they attacked by air.
4 To build large bombers which would be able to fly all the way to Germany.
5 To get better at spotting enemy aircraft by using radar.

It was because of these plans that aircraft such as the Hurricane and Spitfire fighters and Blenheim and Lancaster bombers were made.

Since 1921, there had been a great improvement in the aircraft which were being built. In the First World War, ships had to be protected by other ships. Now, ships could be protected by aeroplanes which could fly hundreds of miles from land.

The Treaty Ports

You read about these on page 8. Britain kept ships at Lough Swilly, Spike Island (near Cork) and Berehaven even after the Free State was set up. They were to help Britain keep enemies out of the Atlantic in case a war broke out again. There were some disadvantages too:

1 Britain didn't have enough money to keep the ports properly. There wasn't enough staff and there were only two ships based at them.
2 The ports depended on getting food from the Free State, so if the Free State decided to stop supporting them this way, there wasn't much Britain could do about it.
3 The Free State didn't want to have British naval bases in its country at all. Britain

knew that if the Irish government wanted to, it could make it very awkward for Britain to use them.

The 1938 agreement

In 1937, **Neville Chamberlain** was the new British Prime Minister. Because it was almost certain that there would be a war, he wanted to try to become more friendly with the Irish Free State in case Britain needed its help.

In 1938 the two governments started to talk about solving some of the problems between them and an agreement was reached. The trade war was ended, although this did not affect trade across the border. Éire paid Britain some money, but it was a lot less than Britain said it should. Britain also agreed to return the three Treaty Ports to Éire, without being sure that they could in fact use them if there was a war. The Free State would have come to some agreement with Britain about being on the same side in a war if Britain would end partition. But Britain refused to do this.

In fact the Free State did well out of these talks, because Chamberlain really wanted to keep de Valera happy in case there was a war with Hitler. He believed that the Free State *would* take Britain's side if war really came.

Below: British troops departing from Spike Island in 1938. Spike Island was on the approaches to Cork.

D

AFTER MOST CAREFUL CONSIDERATION, WE CAME TO THE CONCLUSION THAT A FRIENDLY IRELAND WAS WORTH FAR MORE TO US BOTH IN PEACE AND IN WAR THAN THESE PAPER RIGHTS WHICH COULD ONLY BE EXERCISED AT THE RISK OF MAINTAINING AND PERHAPS INCREASING THEIR SENSE OF GRIEVANCE. . .

(Neville Chamberlain. Speech in the House of Commons, 5 May 1938.)

SOURCE

E

THESE PORTS ARE . . . THE SENTINEL TOWERS OF THE WESTERN APPROACHES. . . NOW WE ARE TO GIVE THEM UP, UNCONDITIONALLY, TO AN IRISH GOVERNMENT LED BY MEN . . . WHOSE RISE TO POWER HAS BEEN PROPORTIONATE TO THE ANIMOSITY WITH WHICH THEY HAVE ACTED AGAINST THIS COUNTRY . . .

(Winston Churchill. Speech in the House of Commons, 5 May 1938.)

SOURCE

?

1 Read all of this unit. Now list the reasons given for (a) giving up the Treaty Ports (b) keeping them.

2 If you had been Chamberlain in 1938, would you have been happy with the agreement reached with the Free State?

Appeasement

In the years 1938 and 1939, Chamberlain, the British Prime Minister, tried to *appease* the dictators Hitler and Mussolini. To *appease* someone means to try to do things that will keep him happy and not annoy him. This way, Britain bought time in which to make its army stronger and get more weapons.

Anschluss with Austria

Now that Hitler had Mussolini on his side — after the Rome-Berlin Axis — he felt more confident. Now he began to plan to increase the power of the German **Third Reich**.

In March 1938 he invaded Austria. Germany and Austria were united. This was called the **Anschluss** and Nazis were given all the important jobs in Austria.

The Czech crisis

Look at the map and you can see that this left Czechoslovakia in a dangerous position. It was surrounded on three sides by German power.

Czechoslovakia was set up as a democracy in 1919 and was made up of four groups of people:

1 The **Czechs** who lived in the west of the country. They did most of the running of the government.
2 A part of Czechoslovakia was called the **Sudetenland**. Three million **Germans** lived here and wanted to be part of Germany.
3 **Slovaks** lived in the west. They wanted their part of the country to be independent.
4 **Ruthenians** lived in the eastern tip. They wanted to be part of Hungary.

Hitler encouraged the Czechs to disagree amongst themselves. He said that the Slovaks and Germans *should* have independent states to themselves.

Chamberlain really didn't want to go to war. He met Hitler several times in 1938 to try to get an agreement. On 29th September 1938, there was a conference in Munich where the leaders of Germany, France, Italy and Britain met. They agreed that Germany should have the Sudetenland. Chamberlain also got Hitler to sign a piece of paper saying that Germany would never go to war with Britain.

The fall of Czechoslovakia

The agreement made in Munich lasted only six months. In **March 1939**, the German army invaded Czechoslovakia. Hitler was able to capture a lot of weapons and some military secrets as well.

Mussolini decided he should keep up with Hitler so in **April 1939**, he invaded Albania.

German troops arriving in the Sudetenland in October 1938.

Poland under threat

There was a part of Poland which divided Germany in two. This was called the **Polish Corridor**. The Nazi's had always wanted to get this piece of land back. Chamberlain knew this and he had a good idea that Hitler would attack Poland next. So he told Poland that Britain would help them if Germany attacked. He also talked to the French and they agreed to work together against Germany if war broke out.

Hitler didn't think that Britain and France were really serious in planning to oppose him. After all the years of appeasement, he thought that Britain and France would not go to war no matter what happened and that they were just bluffing.

The Nazi-Soviet Pact

The only country Hitler was worried about was Russia. So, in **August 1939** Germany and Russia signed an agreement called the **Nazi-Soviet Pact**. According to this pact, Russia agreed to stay neutral when Germany attacked Poland — but in return Russia would get half of Poland.

Hitler thought that Britain and France wouldn't dare do anything to him now, so he **invaded Poland** on **1st September 1939**. He was surprised when Britain and France declared war on him. This was the start of the **Second World War**.

THE TRUTH WAS THAT THE FINANCIAL EFFORT AND THE MILITARY PREPARATIONS UNWITTINGLY CREATED A TIMETABLE THAT WAS VERY DIFFICULT TO ALTER. FROM THE START BRITISH REARMAMENT WAS PLANNED WITH THE IDEA OF A POTENTIAL CONFLICT IN 1939 . . . WAR COULD NOT BE FOUGHT WITH ANY CONFIDENCE IN 1938; BUT NEITHER COULD WAR EASILY BE POSTPONED MUCH BEYOND 1940.
(From **The Road to War** by Richard Overy)

?

1 Study the map. Why do you think Poland was not prepared to give up the **Polish Corridor**?

2 Would the British have found the German joke in Source B funny?

3 Was Britain right to declare war in 1939?

A

B

ALL THE SMALL STATES CAN DO, IF THE STATESMEN OF THE GREATER STATES FAIL IN THEIR DUTY, IS RESOLUTELY TO DETERMINE THAT THEY WILL NOT BECOME THE TOOLS OF ANY GREAT POWER, AND THAT THEY WILL RESIST WITH WHATEVER STRENGTH THEY MAY POSSESS EVERY ATTEMPT TO DRIVE THEM INTO WAR AGAINST THEIR WILL.
(Eamon de Valera, 1936, speaking at Geneva on Irish neutrality.)

De Valera and Chamberlain

Éamonn de Valera and Chamberlain actually got on quite well together. Chamberlain kept hoping that de Valera would agree to side with Britain if war broke out. De Valera hoped that Chamberlain would be so clever in dealing with other countries that there would be no war and he would not have to make any decisions about taking sides.

During 1938 and 1939 de Valera was thinking more about the partition of Ireland and how to end it. He hinted to the British government that Éire might be more helpful to Britain in a war if they gave in and agreed to do away with the border.

Craigavon and Chamberlain

Lord Craigavon was the Prime Minister of Northern Ireland at this time. In January 1938, he called an election in Northern Ireland. His party, the Unionists, won 39 out of the 52 seats. So Craigavon was able to say that Northern Ireland clearly wanted to stay in the United Kingdom. By 1939 Britain was giving more orders to the Belfast shipyards and the new Shorts aircraft factory.

In April 1939, the British government decided to bring in **conscription**. Because there were so many Nationalists in Northern Ireland who would not want to fight for Britain, it was decided not to have conscription there. Craigavon wanted conscription in Northern Ireland as well, but this annoyed the Nationalists.

Chamberlain and Craigavon met in London to talk about it. Lady Craigavon wrote about what happened in her diary. You can read this in Source E.

The IRA campaign of 1939

In January 1939, the IRA gave Britain four days to leave Northern Ireland. When Britain ignored this, the IRA began bombing in England.

The IRA planted over 120 bombs. Their targets were mostly factories and places like telephone exchanges. The worst bomb was in Coventry where six people were killed. De Valera did not support this at all. He was embarrassed by it. The British and Irish governments took on extra powers to help fight the IRA.

SEPT 1939
IRISH ARMED FORCES

7500 REGULAR SOLDIERS
5000 RESERVISTS
7200 VOLUNTEERS
21 ARMOURED VEHICLES
15 TRAINING AIRCRAFT
4 BIPLANE FIGHTERS
6 SPOTTER AIRCRAFT
3 AMPHIBIOUS AIRCRAFT
A FEW TRANSPORT AIRCRAFT

A Sunderland flying boat landing. One similar to this landed near Dublin on the day war broke out.

The outbreak of war

De Valera kept his promise to stay neutral when war broke out. It was a way of pointing out that Éire was not under British control any more and did not have to do what Britain did.

But neutrality was not simple to carry out. The Éire army uniforms looked very like German ones. this would have caused confusion if the Germans had invaded. In 1940, the Irish uniform was changed to look more neutral.

On the day war broke out, a British warplane ran out of fuel and landed off the Irish coast near Dublin. It was quietly refuelled and allowed to take off again.

A lot of German U boats appeared in Irish waters. A big British passenger ship, called the *Athenia*, was sunk by the Germans off the Donegal coast the night after war was declared. Over 100 people died. Many of the crews on British ships which were attacked were in fact Irish, and many Irish people were joining the British army.

Staying neutral was not going to be easy.

E

J. (JAMES) WAS ASKED FLAT OUT BY CHAMBERLAIN, "IS ULSTER OUT TO HELP BRITAIN IN HER WAR EFFORT?" TO WHICH, OF COURSE, HE ANSWERED, "YOU KNOW WE ARE. I HAVE OFFERED PERSONALLY ALL THE RESOURCES AT OUR DISPOSAL TO HELP YOU, AND WE HAVE PASSED RESOLUTIONS IN OUR PARLIAMENT TO THE SAME EFFECT." CHAMBERLAIN SAID, "IF YOU REALLY WANT TO HELP US, **DON'T** PRESS FOR CONSCRIPTION. IT WILL ONLY BE AN EMBARRASSMENT. WHAT ELSE COULD J. DO THAN SAY, "VERY WELL THEN, I WON'T!"

(Lady Craigavon's diary, 2 May 1939)

?

1 Study Source C. Would these forces have been enough to stop a German or British invasion? Explain your answer.

2 Why did Chamberlain not want conscription introduced in Northern Ireland? (Text and Source E)

3 Would it be more difficult for Éire or New Zealand to remain neutral in the war?

2.1 Britain prepares for war, 1939-40

By 1939 Britain was more ready for war than most countries. Although Chamberlain had tried to keep Hitler happy, the government had prepared for war since 1935. You read about this on page 18. By September 1938, the Royal Air Force had six squadrons of the new Hurricane fighters. A year later there were twenty-six.

Military preparations

There was conscription in Britain since April 1939. Radar was a new invention and it could show up German aircraft when they were over thirty miles from the British coast. The RAF could then fly to attack them. New designs of aeroplane were built very quickly and there were dozens of new ships built for the Royal Navy. Anti-aircraft guns, searchlights and barrage balloons were also built.

Civil defence preparations

Chamberlain was afraid of what might happen to ordinary people if the German Luftwaffe began bombing British cities. Plans were made to make sure as few people as possible were hurt.

1 All women and children were to be moved out of the cities as soon as war was declared. This was known as **evacuation**.
2 Air raid shelters were ordered for people to put in their back gardens. When bombs were being dropped, families could hide in these and be protected.
3 Everybody in the country was given a gas mask in case Hitler tried to use poison gas.
4 The **Air Raid Protection** force was formed, known as the **ARP**. These were volunteers who made sure people did not show lights at night which might guide German planes to the cities. This was known as the **black-out**. They also organised rescue efforts when bombs did fall.
5 The government took over control of food supplies, transport and factories. This meant that if there were emergencies because of war, the government had the power to do what it thought was necessary. For example, it might take over an ordinary factory and start making guns in it, or it might need to take over trains or buses to carry troops about.

Preparations in Northern Ireland

The Stormont government thought that Northern Ireland was too far away from Germany to be in any danger. In 1939, Northern Ireland had no RAF fighters to protect it, no searchlights and hardly any anti-aircraft guns. At first, when war broke out, there was a black-out, but as time went on people began to ignore it and laughed at the ARP wardens. Cinemas and dance halls stayed open, and not many people took the chance to be evacuated from Belfast.

The Phoney War

In Britain, as soon as war was declared in September 1939, one and a half million children — that is as many people as live in Northern Ireland — were evacuated from the south of England to country areas where they would be safer. This was a terrible experience for many children. They were separated from their parents and lived with strangers. Sometimes even brothers and sisters were split up.

A

Left: *Children boarding a train to be evacuated from London. A soldier kisses his little son goodbye. All child evacuees had a label to identify them. The square box was the child's gas mask.*

Below: *Various kinds of WW2 air raid shelter on display at Eden Camp military museum, in Yorkshire. Owners erected these in their back gardens. They were buried under soil with steps leading down to the entrance. On the left is an Anderson shelter.*

B

DO NOT GIVE ANY GERMAN ANYTHING. DO NOT TELL HIM ANYTHING. HIDE YOUR FOOD AND YOUR BICYCLES. HIDE YOUR MAPS. SEE THAT THE ENEMY GETS NO PETROL. IF YOU HAVE A CAR OR MOTOR BICYCLE, PUT IT OUT OF ACTION WHEN NOT IN USE. IT IS NOT ENOUGH TO REMOVE THE IGNITION KEY; YOU MUST MAKE IT USELESS TO ANYONE EXCEPT YOURSELF.

IF YOU ARE A GARAGE PROPRIETOR, YOU MUST WORK OUT A PLAN TO PROTECT YOUR STOCK OF PETROL AND YOUR CUSTOMERS' CARS. REMEMBER THAT TRANSPORT AND PETROL WILL BE THE INVADER'S MAIN DIFFICULTIES. MAKE SURE THAT NO INVADER WILL BE ABLE TO GET HOLD OF YOUR CARS, PETROL, MAPS OR BICYCLES.

*Advice from a Ministry of Information leaflet **If the Invader comes**.*

SOURCE

C

1946 PREFAB →

?

1 Read the list of civil defence preparations. Look at Sources A and C *and their captions.* What items on the list do they illustrate?

2 Read Source B. If you owned a garage, what would you have to do to carry out the instructions here?

3 Imagine you are an evacuee from London. Write about what happens and how you feel.

The Phoney War

The first seven months of the Second World War were called 'the phoney war' because the Germans did not try to attack Britain. They were too busy invading Poland.

France did not try to invade Germany either, even though the British Army and the RAF went over to France to be ready for any action. All the RAF dropped on Germany were propaganda leaflets!

Because there wasn't much going on, Britain was able to continue building up its army. The Royal Navy tried to stop Germany getting supplies by **blockading** the North Sea and the Baltic.

During these early stages, German U-boats sank a lot of British ships, mostly in Irish waters.

Hitler's invasion of Western Europe, Spring 1940.

In March 1940, Chamberlain thought that Germany had left it too late to attack Britain. He told the House of Commons: "Hitler has missed the bus".

German iron ore came from northern Sweden, shipped through Norway, so the Royal Navy began to lay mines off Norway to stop any ore getting through to Germany.

Denmark and Norway

The phoney war ended suddenly on **9 April 1940** when Hitler invaded Denmark and Norway. He was surprised to find that the British navy was there when he arrived! There was fierce fighting and the Germans lost a lot of ships. Even so, the Nazis fought back and the British were forced to retreat.

Churchill is made Prime Minister

Chamberlain resigned on 9 May 1940 because he had not foreseen that Hitler might attack Norway. **Winston Churchill** became Prime Minister.

Hitler strikes in the west

The next day, Hitler invaded Holland and Belgium. Parts of the British and French armies which had been in France, were moved into Belgium to stop the Germans.

But the Germans had only been trying to turn attention away from what they really meant to do.

In **Operation Sickle**, the main attack came unexpectedly through the Ardennes forest. Here Hitler's army burst into France on 14 May and France faced disaster.

The Germans were very successful because their tanks moved so fast, and were covered by fighter planes. One type of plane was called the **Stuka** dive bomber. This plane made a screaming sound as it was diving and was a terrifying sound for any soldier to hear.

This tactic used by the Germans was called a **Blitzkrieg**. This means 'lightning war'.

German tanks reached the French coast next to Britain and some parts of the British army were trapped between them and the sea, at the French town of Dunkirk.

The Dunkirk evacuation

The Luftwaffe had completely destroyed the town of Dunkirk so the

5 June 1940: British equipment and bodies on the beaches of Dunkirk, just after the evacuation was completed.

22 June 1940: Hitler and his generals wait beside the famous railway carriage to accept the surrender of France.

soldiers were trapped on the beaches. There was an appeal on British radio for help to save the men at Dunkirk. **Operation Dynamo** began. Anybody who had a yacht, a fishing boat or any kind of boat at all, set off across the channel to join the Royal Navy in trying to rescue the men. Over 1000 boats went, with the RAF trying to protect them from the air. Many ships and boats were sunk, but the operation was a success, with over 300,000 men saved by wading out into the sea to the rescue boats.

But the Germans reached Paris and on 22 June 1940 the French surrendered. France was in German hands, and Britain had lost its most important ally.

An illustration from a wartime children's book, showing Spitfires in combat with Heinkel 111s and Me110s.

"The Battle of France is over. I expect that the Battle of Britain is about to begin."
These words were spoken by Winston Churchill in the House of Commons on 18 June 1940. Britain stood alone against Hitler.

The British army was safely back from Dunkirk but they had had to leave most of their heavy weapons behind. There weren't enough rifles for the ordinary soldiers, let alone the new **Home Guard** — men who weren't in the army but who gave up their spare time to guard the coast against any invasion.

Factories in Britain worked round the clock to make fighter planes. Half a million rifles were bought from the USA.

Hitler planned **Operation Sealion**. This was his plan to destroy the Royal Navy and the Royal Air Force. The coming battle was going to be fought almost entirely in the air. For the first time, Hitler faced an airforce that could really fight back.

Britain was now very glad of all the preparations for war which it had made in the 1930s.

RAF pilots who had to bail out if they were shot down over England, could recover and then go back on duty. If

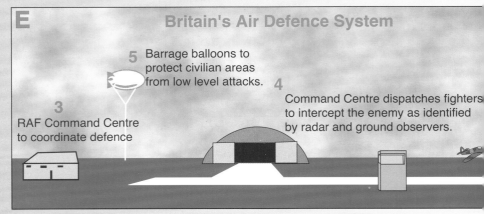

E Britain's Air Defence System

5 Barrage balloons to protect civilian areas from low level attacks.

4 Command Centre dispatches fighters to intercept the enemy as identified by radar and ground observers.

3 RAF Command Centre to coordinate defence

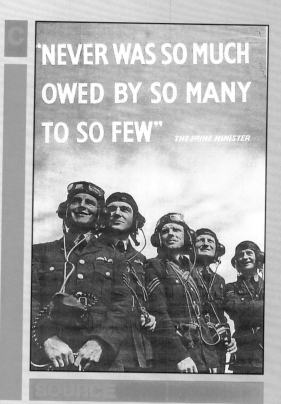

SOURCE C

German pilots did the same, they were captured and couldn't go back to the fighting.

Even so, the RAF was nearly defeated because during August 1940, their planes were being shot down faster than new ones could be built. It was also a very bad time to be a pilot. Pilots were being killed faster than more could be trained to replace them.

The pilots who fought the Battle of Britain in the skies at this time soon became known as **The Few** (see Source B). The future of Britain depended on them winning.

In October 1940, Germany gave up plans to invade Britain, but then **The Blitz** started.

The Luftwaffe flew to Britain every night and bombed cities. This went on until June 1941.

Date	Luftwaffe	RAF
Aug 12	31	22
Aug 13	45	13
Aug 15	55	34
Aug 16	45	21
Aug 18	49	27

Losses of aircraft in the Battle of Britain.

SOURCE D

2 Chain of radar stations on the coast to spot enemy aircraft while still over the sea. Ground observers identify type, number and altitude. RAF Command Centre alerted.

1 Approaching enemy aircraft are picked up by radar often before they have crossed the French coast.

The first big bombing raid on London was on 7 September 1940. The docks were attacked and set on fire by 320 bombers. There were 430 people killed and 1600 seriously injured.

London was bombed *every night* between 7 September and 2 November 1940. The city was bombed, but not quite so often, right up to June 1941. This time became known as **The Blitz**.

The RAF was able to keep the bombers away during the day, but at night time, Londoners got very used to air-raid sirens going off, and hearing the sound of the anti-aircraft guns firing as they made their way to the air-raid shelters.

The stations of the Underground railway were used as bomb shelters also.

It wasn't easy for the soldiers firing the anti-aircraft guns at night. They were afraid they might shoot down one of their own planes in the dark. One night they decided not to use the guns and to leave the RAF planes free to attack the German bombers. The ordinary people could hear only the sound of aircraft and falling bombs. They didn't like not being able to hear the guns fighting back. So the next night the guns started to fire again.

Other big British cities were bombed in the Blitz. In November 1940, 544 people were killed in a German raid on Coventry.

Throughout the long winter of 1940-41, Ulster was left alone by the German planes. Then, in April 1941, the Germans came to Belfast.

A

THE SLEEP DISTURBER — by Illingworth.

Daily Mail, March 1941. A rather optimistic view of the effects of ground defenses on German bombers. In reality anti aircraft gunners expended 180,000 shells for every aircraft brought down.

SOURCE

B

CITY	RAIDS	KILLED	INJURED	HOUSES DAMAGED OR DESTROYED
BELFAST	4	955	2436	56,885
COVENTRY	43	1251	1859	54,373
HULL	82	c1200	c1800	86,722
SOUTHAMPTON	57	633	1908	43,289
PORTSMOUTH	67	930	2837	13,174

SOURCE Air raid casualties in some British cities

At first, people in Northern Ireland did not really believe that the Germans would bomb the province. Some even thought that Irish neutrality meant that the Germans would leave the North alone too.

Belfast had only 22 anti-aircraft guns and there was space in the shelters for only a quarter of the people in the city. There were only a few fighter planes for protection.

But Belfast had become important as a place for building aircraft and other equipment needed in the war. In fact German aircraft had been spotted spying over Belfast and Derry.

A member of the Stormont government asked London for more guns. He said that he was afraid that the new moon in April 1941 would mean that it was Northern Ireland's turn to be bombed.

He was right. The German pilots liked to fly when there was a full moon.

The Raids

There were four raids by the Luftwaffe in Belfast. These were in April and May 1941. The Germans started with a small attack, probably just to test out how well Belfast was defended.

Easter Tuesday, 15-16 April

This was a cloudless night. The Germans came in from the Irish Sea, over Newtownards. There were nearly 200 bombers. By the next morning 745 people were dead.

C *Blitz damage at Eglinton Street, near Carlisle Circus.*

D AT THE TIME OF THE BIG RAID ON 15/16 APRIL 1941, I WAS LIVING ON THE CASTLEREAGH ROAD IN BELFAST. I WAS A MEMBER OF THE ATS AND, ALTHOUGH NOT ON DUTY THAT NIGHT, I WENT OUT AND TO SEE WHAT I COULD DO TO HELP RESCUE PEOPLE. I SPENT THE WHOLE NIGHT HELPING TO PUT OUT FIRES, AND FILLING SANDBAGS. IT WAS AN EXHAUSTING NIGHT AND WHEN THE 'ALL-CLEAR' CAME NEXT MORNING, MY THOUGHTS TURNED TO MY MOTHER, WHO LIVED IN JELLICOE AVENUE.

I HAD HEARD THAT THE ANTRIM ROAD AREA HAD BEEN BADLY HIT, AND WITH MY HEART IN MY MOUTH I HURRIED THERE ON FOOT — THERE WERE NO BUSES OR TRAMS DUE TO THE BOMBING. WHEN I GOT THERE, I FOUND THAT A PARACHUTE MINE HAD LANDED AT THE TOP OF GLANDORE AVENUE, NEAR MY MOTHER'S, KILLING MANY PEOPLE, BUT MY MOTHER'S HOUSE WAS UNSCATHED. WHEN I ENTERED THE HOUSE SHE HAD THE VACUUM CLEANER OUT, CLEARING SOOT OFF THE SITTING ROOM CARPET. HER FIRST WORDS WERE: "LOOK AT THE MESS THOSE GERMANS HAVE MADE OF MY NICE CLEAN CARPET"!

Kathleen Twist, Staff Sergeant Major ATS, April 1941

SOURCE

The raid had started fires all over the city and the firemen could hardly cope. Someone in the Stormont government phoned Dublin and asked de Valera for help. He sent thirteen fire engines to Belfast to work alongside the Belfast firemen.

May 4-5, 1941

This was another big raid and by the time the German bombers had finished, 150 people had been killed and Belfast harbour and shipyards were a raging inferno. German pilots could see the fires from England.

The Antrim Road on the morning after the raid on 15/16 April 1941. These houses were just opposite St James Church.

7-8 May 1941

This was a smaller raid, where fourteen people were killed.

The Blitz ended when Germany invaded Russia in June 1941. In Belfast there had been nearly 1000 people killed and over half the houses in the city were damaged or wrecked.

F

A LARGE AIR-RAID SHELTER IN PERCY STREET (SHANKHILL ROAD END) WAS FULL. A LAND MINE FLOATED DOWN BY PARACHUTE AND IT RECEIVED A DIRECT HIT, KILLING EVERYONE IN IT.

I WAS EMPLOYED AS 2ND CLASS SWIMMING-BATH ATTENDANT ON THE FALLS ROAD. THE POOL WAS EMPTIED AND OVER A HUNDRED BODIES WERE BROUGHT IN AND LAID OUT.

ONE COFFIN CONTAINED (ALL OPEN) A YOUNG MOTHER WITH HER TWO DEAD CHILDREN, ONE IN EACH ARM.

From the memories of Sydney Coleshill, Belfast, April 1941.

?

Unit 2.2

1 Write diary entries describing what happened on the following days: 9 April 1940; 9 May 1940; 22 June 1940.

Unit 2.3

2 Do you think it is fair to say that, in 1940, the pilots of the RAF saved Britain all by themselves?

Unit 2.4

3 Why do you think the Luftwaffe thought it was worth bombing Belfast? Give all the reasons you can think of.

Prospective volunteers outside the Central Recruiting Office, Clifton Street, North Belfast.

All through the war, Britain had conscription, where all men who were able to fight had to join the army. After a while, there was conscription for unmarried women too. The posters on the right show some of the organisations which women could join. They could also work in factories or in the country as **land girls**. Land girls helped on the farms which were producing food for the country. During the war there were so many men away fighting, that women took over many of their jobs.

Northern Ireland did not have conscription because Nationalists were against it (see page 22). However, many people from the province did join up voluntarily. The Prime Minister, Craigavon, was pleased because he was anxious that Northern Ireland should not show up badly against the rest of the country. He had told Britain that Northern Ireland would play a full part in the war.

As the war went on, fewer and fewer people joined the army. Many young men from Ulster had been killed in the First World War, and the memory of this was very painful.

?

1 Why do you think the Government wanted women in the armed services?

2 How important was farming during the war?

SOURCES

> WE WERE ALONE AND HAD TO FACE SINGLE-HANDED THE FULL FURY OF THE GERMAN ATTACKS ... SEEKING TO STRANGLE OUR LIFE BY CUTTING OFF THE ENTRY TO OUR PORTS ... . ONLY ONE GREAT CHANNEL OF ENTRY REMAINED OPEN. THAT CHANNEL REMAINED OPEN BECAUSE LOYAL ULSTER GAVE US FULL USE OF THE NORTH IRISH PORTS AND WATERS ... . BUT FOR ITS LOYALTY ... WE SHOULD HAVE BEEN CONFRONTED WITH SLAVERY AND DEATH.
>
> *Winston Churchill, in a letter to JM Andrews, 6 May 1943.*

SOURCE

The Battle of the Atlantic

For Britain, one of the most important battles in the Second World War was the **Battle of the Atlantic**. German U-boats attacked and sank merchant ships which were carrying supplies to Britain. Britain had to have these supplies, so if Germany could stop them then there was no hope for Britain.

Londonderry

Northern Ireland, and particularly the City of Derry, became very important in the Battle of the Atlantic. Merchant ships came across the Atlantic in **convoys**. Each convoy was protected on its journey by up to nine warships. Derry was the biggest base in the United Kingdom for these warships.

Before the war, most ships coming to Britain came round the *South* of Ireland. When the Germans took over France in 1940, it became too dangerous for ships to go that way. So after 1940, ships went to the *North* of Ireland. Derry was the biggest port close to this route. Only two bombs were dropped on Derry during the war, but they killed 13 people at **Messines Park**.

The naval base

The port at Derry had to get a lot bigger. A big wharf was built at **Lisahally**, near the city. Five army camps and a hospital were also set up.

When the USA joined in the war on the Allied (Britain's) side, a huge number of American ships had to be kept at Derry as well. All the people who worked on these ships came with them, of course. At this time, there were nearly twice as many people living in Derry as there had been before the war.

Magee College

At Magee College in Derry there was a secret bunker set up which could take over from England if their headquarters there, looking after the **Western Approaches**, was bombed.

Ballykelly airbase

Ballykelly and Eglinton were two important air bases in the North-West. At Ballykelly , a railway line crossed the runway! Signals stopped aeroplanes when a train was due (see picture D, opposite).

U-boats at Lisahally, 1945

When Germany surrendered at the end of the war, all U-boats had to surface to show they had stopped fighting. Forty-three of them were brought up the Foyle to Lisahally.

?

1 Are there any ways in which the war was *good* for Derry?

2 Imagine you are a German sailor on the U-boat in Source F opposite. Describe how you feel as you sail into Culmore.

Top left: British sailors at Derry greet the arrival of the US destroyer **USS Dallas** in 1942.

Top right: Bomb damage caused by a German parachute mine at Messines Park, Derry, 16 April 1941.

Left: A Liberator bomber waiting for a train to pass over the runway at Ballykelly.

Right: British warships moored alongside the quays at Derry, during the war.

Below left: The surrender of German U-boats in May 1945. Local people at Culmore watching the arrival of U-1009.

Below Right: Surrendered U-boats moored at Lisahally.

A

Castle Archdale flying boat base viewed from the air. Today this is a popular tourist area and caravan park. The large house that gave the base its name can be seen among the trees. The base is still under construction in this photo. Note the Sunderlands in for servicing. They were placed on wheels for this purpose. (See also map, page 40.)

B

RAF crew on the pier at Castle Archdale, 5 March 1945, waiting for a boat to take them out to their aircraft.

C

JUST LIKE SOME WAYWARD PRODIGALS
THEIR LIFE TO START ANEW
BACK TO CASTLE ARCHDALE CAME
THE MEN OF 422

WE DIDN'T MIND THE RAIN AND MUD
FERMANAGH ISN'T DEVON
BUT AFTER WHAT WE'D SEEN LAST YEAR
LOUGH ERNE WAS SIMPLY HEAVEN

Poem by a Canadian airman.

SOURCE

Coastal Command

The Royal Air Force Coastal Command played an important part in the Battle of the Atlantic. They gave air cover to the warships which were escorting convoys. They could also fire at German U-boats. The RAF sank nearly as many U-boats as the navy did. Because of where it was, Ulster was a very good place for air bases. There were eight main air bases set up — Aldergrove, Nutts Corner, Long Kesh, which were all near Belfast; Eglinton, Ballykelly and Limavady which were in Co Londonderry, and Killadeas and Castle Archdale which were in Co Fermanagh.

Castle Archdale

Castle Archdale, at Lough Erne, was the perfect place for **flying boats**. A flying boat is an aeroplane which can take off or land on water. Lough Erne had deep calm water, and it was also near the west coast.

The planes had to land in daylight because there were so many mountains that it was too dangerous to land in the dark.

An Atlantic convoy being escorted by Coastal Command, RAF. The nearest aircraft is a Sunderland flying boat. Behind it are two Ansons and in the distance a Walrus flying boat. Sunderlands were built in Belfast and based at Castle Archdale, among other places. Note the four-funnelled Royal Navy destroyer and the cruiser.

If you look at the map on page 40 you will see that, to fly to Castle Archdale from the Atlantic, aeroplanes had to fly over south Donegal. This was part of Éire and Éire was neutral in the war. The Éire government allowed the RAF and the United States Air Force to fly over this part of their country. This meant that, in this case, they *were* taking sides. If this had not been allowed, there would have been no point in having a flying boat base at Castle Archdale.

There was a special flying boat dock built at Castle Archdale where Sunderland flying boats could be serviced without having to be taken out of the water. This dock is still there and might be the only flying boat dock left in the world.

Some Canadian planes were based at Castle Archdale too. One Canadian pilot wrote a poem which you can read in Source C.

The Bismarck

A famous event happened at Castle Archdale when a plane from there, called a Catalina, spotted the German warship, *Bismarck*, in the Atlantic. The pilots of the Catalina were able to tell the Royal Navy where it was and they sank it.

?

1 Using Sources A, B and C and the text on these two pages, write a letter to a friend in the RAF describing Castle Archdale and what it is like to be a pilot based there.

2 Using the text in this chapter and the map on page 40, explain why Lough Erne was a good base for the flying boats.

During the Second World War the British government took control of the country and its people in a way that is hard to imagine today. This chapter tells you how they did this.

Food

Britain **imported** a lot of food from other countries. German U-boats tried to sink ships bringing in food, so a **Ministry of Food** was set up to make sure that as much food as possible was grown in the country and that nothing was wasted. Farmers were encouraged to grow more and ordinary people were told to grow more in their own gardens. Vegetables were grown on land that you wouldn't usually think of growing anything on — like railway embankments. The lawns in front of Queen's University in Belfast were used for growing vegetables.

Foods such as meat, sugar, butter, eggs and bread were **rationed**. Oranges and bananas were very hard to get. Eating carrots was supposed to give you good eyesight. People said that pilots who flew at night were fed a lot of carrots!

The government helped to pay for children to have milk every day at school, and to have school meals. Although this all seems strange today, it was actually a very healthy diet. Children were fed better than they had been before the war.

Prices and wages

Because so many things were hard to get, prices went up. However, wages went up as well, so people weren't too badly off. As you can imagine, farmers did particularly well. Taxes were very high. Income tax today is 24%. In 1945 it was 50%.

Posters issued by the Ministry of Food to encourage good eating habits and avoid waste.

An Illingworth cartoon in the Daily Mail, April 1941, showing Ernest Bevin (Minister of Labour) encouraging people to work in the factories.

IN DELAY THERE LIES NO PLENTY; THEN COME - ER - HELP ME SWEET - AND - TWENTY...

WAR INDUSTRIES

Willie Moore, from Lisnaskea, Co Fermanagh in his Local Defence Volunteer (Home Guard) uniform, in 1940. This should be compared with that on page 42.

Employment

As many people as possible helped to produce materials and equipment that were needed in the war. Most of the men were away in the army, so women became very important workers. In 1941, unmarried women were conscripted. They could choose to join a women's armed force, or to work in a factory, or they could become **land girls**, helping on the farms while the men were away.

The Home Guard

Have you seen the television programme called *Dad's Army,* about Captain Mainwaring and his platoon? This was a comedy programme about the Home Guard. Although this programme was funny, it was supposed to be very like the real Home Guard. It performed a very important job of guarding the coast in case of invasion. It also guarded important buildings.

Many of those in the Home Guard were older men who had fought in the First World War, or boys who were too young to join the army — like Private Pike in *Dad's Army*!.

There was a Home Guard in Northern Ireland. At first they wore dark grey uniforms like the one the man in Source F is wearing. Later on they got khaki uniforms like the one on page 42.

?

1 Using the information in this chapter, describe the difficulties which people faced during the war.

2 Look at Sources A, B, C, D and E. Which ones are trying to get a message over to children?

3 Who do you think Source E is asking to work in factories?

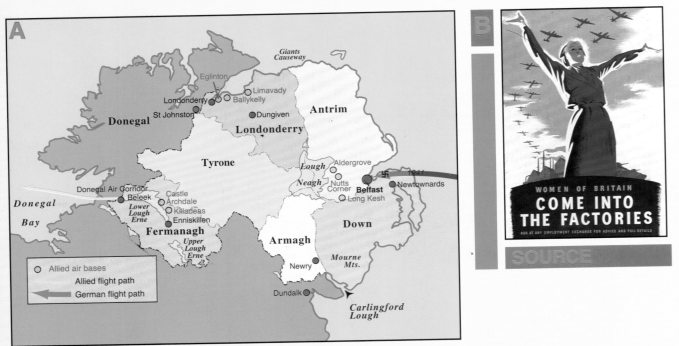

Northern Ireland"s experience of war was different from the UK's in some ways.

Industry

In England factories were working very hard to make equipment for the army and air force. New factories were built and there was hardly any unemployment.

At first there were no new factories built in Northern Ireland, and unemployment was high. This was partly because there was no conscription, but it was also because the government at Stormont was very slow to prepare Northern Ireland for the war. The aircraft factory of Short Brothers and Harland took three times as long to build an aeroplane as the factories in England. The British government was worried about this.

The United States joined the war in December 1941. American troops, warships and aircraft began to arrive in Northern Ireland and unemployment fell.

In 1943, **Sir Basil Brooke** was appointed Prime Minister of Northern Ireland. He was Prime Minister until 1963. Under his leadership, Northern Ireland began to help more in the effort to win the war.

Harland and Wolff

Northern Ireland gave a lot towards winning the war. The shipyards were particularly busy. They built 140 warships and 123 merchant ships. They also made 500 tanks. During the worst of the war, nearly 36,000 people worked in the shipyards.

Short and Harland

The two main types of aircraft built at Short and Harland's aircraft factory in Belfast were Stirling bombers and Sunderland flying boats. Some of these can be seen in the picture opposite. The factory also repaired damaged planes.

Textiles

The linen factories in Ulster made 30 million shirts, nearly all that were needed for

Short Stirling bombers (foreground) and Sunderland flying boats (left) at Queen's Island, Belfast, January 1944.

James Magennis, VC.

the whole British Army. Linen was also used to make 2 million parachutes.

Other industries

Other things made in Ulster were bayonets, shells, bullets and camouflage nets. A third of all rope used by the army was made in Ulster.

Agriculture

Right from the start of the war, Northern Ireland's agriculture did very well. More land was ploughed up to grow crops instead of being left for grazing or hay. Linen is made from flax, so farmers grew six times more flax during the war than before.

Ulster supplied a fifth of the eggs needed in the whole of the United Kingdom. Its farmers also supplied sheep and cattle and sent thousands of litres of milk to Scotland every day.

James Magennis, VC

James Magennis was the only person from Northern Ireland to win the Victoria Cross for bravery. He was from the Donegal Road area of Belfast. In July 1945 he had attached six limpet mines to a Japanese ship near Borneo. The mines destroyed the ship. He used a midget submarine and could have been spotted and killed at any time during the thirty minutes it took to do the job. His medal was presented by King George VI, but there was little fuss made about it in Northern Ireland.

Not nearly so many people from Northern Ireland were killed in the Second World War as had been killed in the First. Not counting those who died in the Blitz and merchant seamen, 4211 people in the armed forces died.

The factories and army and navy bases in the province were of great importance in the effort to win the war.

?

1 Do you think that Northern Ireland's contribution to the war effort was very important? Explain why you think this.

2 Describe the life of (a) a farmer (b) a dock worker in Northern Ireland during the war.

2.10 ULSTER DURING THE WAR

On the whole, Britain suffered more than Ulster did during the war, but a lot of things did change in the province.

Food supplies

There was more food in Ulster than in Britain. There were always plenty of vegetables and bacon and pork were not rationed. Because of this soldiers, especially Americans, were often sent to Ulster for training. Some things, like sugar, tea and fruit from other countries, were scarce and later in the war even eggs were hard to get.

Blackout regulations

Pilots of enemy aircraft could see a city if there was a lot of light showing at night. To keep the light from showing, people had to use heavy curtains on their windows. Cars, buses and bicycles had to put hoods over their lights so that only a very little light showed. White strips were painted on bumpers to try to help, but there were a lot of accidents.

Victor Stronge in his Home Guard uniform, outside his lodgings in Coleraine. In May 1945 he travelled to Lisahally to see the surrendered German U-boats and was allowed to board one.

Transport

Because there was so little petrol, only people like doctors were allowed to have any. Many car owners took the wheels off their cars and stored them until it was all over. Milk men had to give up their vans and go back to using a horse and cart. Because so few people could use cars, they used buses and trains instead. Even the buses had to make sure they did not waste fuel, so the last bus was about 7.00pm. If you were out at night you had to walk or cycle home. Trains weren't so short of fuel because they used coal. So the railway became a very important way of getting about. The line from Belfast to Londonderry, via Coleraine, was very busy.

Cross-border smuggling

Because Éire was neutral, you could get a lot of things there that you couldn't get in Northern Ireland. So sometimes people tried to smuggle things like butter, meat and sugar across the border. This took place especially along the Fermanagh border and also across Carlingford Lough.

There are many stories about this smuggling, when smugglers tried to outwit the RUC and customs men. One winter, a rather fat lady was invited by a customs man to warm herself by his roaring fire while he checked her shopping. When he came back she was a much thinner lady and there was a pool of melted butter at her feet!

The military presence

One very noticeable thing in Ulster was the number of men and women who were in the army. There were thousands and thousands of them. Most of the time, the local people and the soldiers got on very well, but sometimes they didn't. Local men were sometimes not pleased that their womenfolk thought men in uniform were very

SMARTEST ATS IN BRITAIN.

NORTHERN IRELAND HAS TAKEN THE LEAD IN THE ATS MOVEMENT IN THE BRITISH ISLES, HAVING THE UNIQUE DISTINCTION OF INCLUDING AMONG ITS MEMBERS THE SMARTEST AND MOST IMMACULATE GIRL THE CHIEF CONTROLLER (MRS JEAN KNOX) HAS EVER SEEN, AND THE SMARTEST SHE HAS INSPECTED AT A RECEPTION DEPOT. BOTH BELONG TO BELFAST IN WHICH THEY WERE BORN.

THE HONOUR OF BEING THE SMARTEST ATS GOES TO MRS M KATHLEEN TWIST, 27 YEAR OLD WIFE OF MR WESLEY TWIST, WHO IS SERVING WITH AN ARTILLERY UNIT IN ENGLAND, AND PRIOR TO THE WAR WAS AN ARCHITECT IN THE MINISTRY OF FINANCE.

SOURCE Belfast Telegraph, 20 October 1941

Kathleen and Wesley Twist in 1940. The photograph was taken during the seven days leave Wesley got after returning from France in June 1940, where his mobile anti-aircraft battery had helped defend Paris from the Luftwaffe. Kathleen is in her Auxiliary Territorial Service (ATS) uniform.

attractive! American soldiers were very popular and nearly 2000 Ulster women married American soldiers whom they met during the war.

The IRA

The IRA caused a lot of problems for the Stormont government during the war. In some Republican parts of Belfast, slogans were painted on the walls. Some of these slogans showed that the IRA did not support Britain in the war, and some even supported Germany. Some slogans said "Up Hitler".

On page 22, you read that the IRA had started to plant bombs in Britain in 1939. Internment was brought in, but the IRA carried out some raids and planted some bombs in Ulster.

Both the British and Irish governments thought that the IRA would stage a rising as soon as the Germans invaded Britain.

The IRA did not like the American soldiers coming after the United States joined the war in 1941. They thought that having British soldiers in Northern Ireland was bad enough without having American ones as well.

Doings of Larry O'Hooligan

ULSTER HAS PRODUCED THE SMARTEST A.T.S GIRL — BUT IT HAD AN OFF-DAY WHEN IT PRODUCED YOU!

THE SERGEANT TAKES A POOR VIEW OF LARRY.

SOURCE Belfast Telegraph, 20/11/41

Sunderland flying boats over Beleek in 1945 on their way back to Castle Archdale. The photo is of the last ever flight over Éire airspace, which was part of the secret 1941 agreement between Britain and Éire.

Before you read these two pages, you should go back and read pages 16–19 and 22–23 again.

The danger of invasion

When Germany captured France in June 1940, it looked more and more likely that Germany would invade Britain and Ireland. The British government really wanted Éire to enter the war on their side. They told de Valera that, if Éire entered the war, they would do away with the border and reunite Ireland very soon. Lord Craigavon was furious about this idea, but de Valera turned down the offer anyway. Probably he thought that Britain was going to lose the war and that Germany would reunite Ireland when they won.

IT IS REMARKABLE HOW EVEN THE ' PRO-BRITISH GROUP', MEN WHO HAVE FOUGHT FOR THE CROWN AND ARE ANXIOUS TO BE CALLED UP AGAIN, MEN WHOSE SONS ARE AT THE FRONT TODAY, LOYALISTS IN THE OLD SENSE OF THE WORD, AGREE GENERALLY IN SUPPORTING THE POLICY OF NEUTRALITY FOR ÉIRE. THEY SEE NO POSSIBLE ALTERNATIVE.
Sir John Maffey, British representative in Ireland, 1939.

SOURCE

Operation Green

Both Germany and Britain considered invading Éire. Churchill still wanted to get the treaty ports back and some members of the army said Britain should take them by force and use them as defence against Germany. This seemed to be too drastic so plans were made to invade the South only if the Germans *actually landed*. Hitler thought that an invasion of Éire would lead to the end of the war. The Germans had a plan to land on the south coast of Ireland. They called this plan **Operation Green**.

"GOD BLESS EIRE'S NEUTRALITY – UNTIL THE FUHRER GETS THERE"

?

Unit 2.10

1 On pages 42 and 43, you read about how difficult things were during the war. Can you think of any *good* things about life then?

Unit 2.11

2 On the whole, was it good or bad for Britain that Éire was neutral during the war?

However, it would have been very difficult to do because Germany did not have control of the sea. In 1941, the Germans considered dropping soldiers on Northern Ireland during the night. They were to land between Belfast and Lough Neagh. They gave up this plan also and by 1942 both sides had given up the idea of invading Ireland.

The Donegal air corridor

You saw that, during the Battle of the Atlantic (pages 34–37), aircraft were based in Northern Ireland to protect convoys of ships which were sailing in the Atlantic. This was possible because of a secret deal between Britain and de Valera. This deal allowed British and American aircraft to fly over Co Donegal to get to and from the Atlantic. This was known as the **Donegal Air Corridor**. On one occasion a fighter plane crashed in fog on the top of Ben Bulben, near Sligo. The remains of it are still there.

The USA in the war

De Valera had thought that America would stay neutral. When America entered the war in 1941 it was even more awkward for Éire to be neutral. The American President at the time was Roosevelt. American troops arrived in Ulster to defend it in January 1942. De Valera protested to the Americans, saying they were interfering in his country. The Americans pointed out that de Valera had not protested to Germany when *they* had bombed Belfast and killed people whom de Valera thought of as Irish citizens.

Benevolent neutrality

Looking back, it is hard to see how Éire could have done anything else during the war. If de Valera had declared war on Germany, Hitler would have been much more likely to invade. Éire *did* act in Britain's favour several times. Allied airmen who crashed in Éire were allowed to return to their own country, but Germans were taken prisoner. During the Blitz on Belfast, firemen from the South helped out. Thousands of Irish citizens joined the British Army and hundreds of them won medals for bravery.

Even though Éire was neutral in the war, it was so close to it that it couldn't help being affected. The Southern government called this time **The Emergency**. The Southern parliament, the Dáil, passed the **Emergency Powers Act** which gave it special powers to deal with the unusual things that were happening.

Shortages

Many things in Éire were very hard to get in the early years of the war. This was because a lot of supplies came into the country by ship, and many of these ships were British. Britain needed its ships for the war and wasn't too keen to spare any to help out a country which was neutral.

It looks like the Germans but it isn't! It is actually an Irish Army patrol mounting a checkpoint on a bridge in 1940. Shortly afterwards the Irish army switched to a less confusing uniform.

Most coal came from Britain, but Britain needed all its coal during the war. So there was hardly any coal in Éire, and most people used turf instead.

Railway engines in those days were run by steam and so needed a lot of coal. The only railway company which had enough coal was the Great Northern Railway which ran between Dublin and Belfast. The North had plenty of coal. When a train was coming from Dublin, two engines were put on it. The second engine stopped at Newry and filled up with coal. Then it went back South and ran some trains there! Later in the war, turf was used on the trains. On some routes there was only one train a week.

Irish Shipping Company

The Éire government set up a **Ministry of Supplies** to try to help get items which were scarce. The Irish Shipping Company was formed , but it could find only a few old ships which it could use. Even these weren't safe because the Germans often fired on neutral ships in the Atlantic.

Rationing

Éire had a lot more food than Britain had, but any food that was imported — like tea, sugar and wheat — was scarce. Instead, sugar was made from sugar beet, which could be grown in Ireland. Although wheat was also grown, farmers couldn't get enough fertilizer, so the crops were not very good. People were allowed only half an ounce (about 1½ grams) of tea and half a pound of sugar a week. Electricity and gas were also rationed. Many factories had to close.

Cross-border trade

Anything which was cheaper on one side of the border was smuggled to the other side. There was no black-out in the South and their cinemas and theatres stayed open, so richer people from the North were able to go south for entertainment.

There were plenty of butter, eggs and meat in the South and so people in the army crossed the border sometimes, although they were not allowed to go in uniform because Éire was neutral. The same rules applied to Germans, so it was possible for a British sailor to meet a German from a U-boat in a Dublin pub!

Éire citizens at war

Even though their country was neutral, many people in Éire joined the British armed forces, or served in the merchant navy. Going to work in a British factory making weapons was a way of getting a job. Thousands also crossed the border to work in Northern Ireland. Many Southern Irish citizens were killed fighting in the war.

In May 1941, thirty-four people were killed and 300 houses destroyed or damaged when German bombs were dropped on North Strand, Dublin. The German pilots had got lost and probably meant to bomb Cardiff instead.

Defence measures

Because either Germany or Britain might invade, the army was made nearly six times bigger. There was also a reserve force set up, and Local Defence Volunteers, but many of these did not even have rifles. The navy and airforce had very little equipment either. If Germany had invaded, Éire would have needed Britain to defend it.

The IRA

There was danger that the IRA might support an invasion by Germany. In December 1939, the IRA raided an army store in Dublin and stole over a million rounds of ammunition. Most of it was found, but fifty IRA members were interned. The government was afraid that, if the IRA was too sympathetic to Germany, it might give the British an excuse to invade.

B

A sailor on an Irish motor torpedo boat practises using the vessel's heavy machine gun.

?

1 What do you think would have happened if (a) Germany or (b) Britain had invaded the South?

2 Do you think life in the South was harder or easier than in the North during the war? Why?

3 Imagine you are a customs officer on duty at a border post in 1943. Describe some of the people you might meet during the day.

The Second World War ended in 1945. Germany surrendered in May and Japan in September.

Since 1943, the Russians had been fighting Germans successfully in the east. In June 1944, the western allies invaded France and began to defeat the Germans in western Europe.

Hitler wouldn't surrender. On 29 April 1945 he committed suicide in Berlin. A week later Germany surrendered.

VE Day in Belfast, 8 May 1945. Crowds outside the City Hall listening to the broadcast of Churchill's victory speech.

Anne Frank, aged 13, at her home in Amsterdam. She was born at Frankfurt, Germany in 1929 and died at Belsen concentration camp in April 1945.

As the allied troops made their way through Europe, they discovered the dreadful **concentration camps** in which the Germans had put Jewish people. The Germans wanted to kill all Jews. They put them to death in these camps, or else they died from disease and starvation. Troops from Northern Ireland were among those which found Belsen camp. Anne Frank was a Jewish girl who died in Belsen. She wrote a diary of her wartime experiences. After she died her diary was published and it has become very famous. She died just a few weeks before the camp was freed.

De Valera's sympathy visit

After Hitler died, de Valera visited the German representative in Dublin to offer his sympathy. He did this after the world knew about the dreadful things that the Germans had done in the concentration camps. He felt that he was keeping up the neutrality of his country right to the end. He had sent his sympathy to the United States when their president had died, and he felt he should do the same for Germany.

The American and British governments were greatly annoyed that anyone should offer sympathy on the death of Hitler who had brought so much misery and death to innocent people. So Éire's neutrality caused annoyance once more.

OWING TO THE ACTION OF MR DE VALERA, SO MUCH AT VARIANCE WITH THE TEMPER AND INSTINCT OF THOUSANDS OF SOUTHERN IRISHMEN WHO HASTENED TO THE BATTLE-FRONT TO PROVE THEIR ANCIENT VALOUR, THE APPROACHES WHICH THE SOUTHERN IRISH PORTS AND AIRFIELDS COULD SO EASILY HAVE GUARDED WERE CLOSED BY THE HOSTILE AIRCRAFT AND U-BOATS. THIS WAS INDEED A DEADLY MOMENT IN OUR LIFE, AND IF IT HAD NOT BEEN FOR THE LOYALTY AND FRIENDSHIP OF NORTHERN IRELAND WE SHOULD HAVE BEEN FORCED TO COME TO CLOSE QUARTERS WITH MR DE VALERA OR PERISH FOR EVER FROM THE EARTH. HOWEVER WITH A RESTRAINT AND POISE TO WHICH, I SAY, HISTORY WILL FIND FEW PARALLELS, HIS MAJESTY'S GOVERNMENT NEVER LAID A VIOLENT HAND UPON THEM, THOUGH AT TIMES IT WOULD HAVE BEEN QUITE EASY AND QUITE NATURAL, AND WE LEFT THE DE VALERA GOVERNMENT TO FROLIC WITH THE GERMANS AND LATER WITH THE JAPANESE REPRESENTATIVES TO THEIR HEART'S CONTENT.

From a speech by Winston Churchill, 13 May 1945.

I KNOW THE KIND OF ANSWER I AM EXPECTED TO MAKE. I KNOW THE ANSWER THAT SPRINGS TO THE LIPS OF EVERY MAN OF IRISH BLOOD WHO HEARD OR READ THAT SPEECH . . . I KNOW THE REPLY I WOULD HAVE GIVEN A QUARTER OF A CENTURY AGO. . . . THERE ARE HOWEVER SOME THINGS WHICH IT IS MY DUTY TO SAY . . . MR CHURCHILL MAKES IT CLEAR THAT, IN CERTAIN CIRCUMSTANCES, HE WOULD HAVE VIOLATED OUR NEUTRALITY AND THAT HE WOULD JUSTIFY HIS ACTION BY BRITAIN'S NECESSITY. IT SEEMS STRANGE TO ME THAT MR CHURCHILL DOES NOT SEE THAT THIS, IF ACCEPTED, WOULD MEAN THAT BRITAIN'S NECESSITY WOULD BECOME A MORAL CODE AND THAT WHEN THIS NECESSITY BECAME SUFFICIENTLY GREAT, OTHER PEOPLE'S RIGHTS WERE NOT TO COUNT.

Éamon de Valera's reply to Winston Churchill, 16 May 1945.

VE Day, 8 May 1945

Churchill declared that the day after Germany surrendered was to be called **Victory in Europe Day**. In Northern Ireland, there were great celebrations, with bonfires, street parties and a two day holiday. A huge crowd gathered at Belfast City Hall to hear a broadcast of Churchill's victory speech.

Churchill and de Valera

Churchill made another speech in which he attacked Éire for not helping in the war. He pointed out how willing Northern Ireland had been to help and how important that help had been. De Valera was greatly annoyed by this and gave a careful reply.

The effects of the war

After the war, Britain felt much more loyal to Northern Ireland and not so friendly to the South. Before, Britain might have done away with the border in order to get the treaty ports back. Now, they were grateful and realised how important the province had been.

?

1 Why were the British and American governments so annoyed when de Valera visited the German minister in Dublin in 1945?

2 Read Source C. What parts of this speech could make you think that Churchill thought Britain might have had to invade Éire?

FRANKENSTEIN

A cartoon dating from the 1945 election. During the war the state had controlled all aspects of life — work, food, housing, production, etc. Labour wanted to retain this control after the war.

SOURCE

Clement Attlee, Prime Minister of Britain from 1945 to 1951.

In July 1945 the long struggle of the Second World War was nearly over. It had cost a great deal in both money and lives. Many, many thousands of people had died. The British government had also run out of money and had had to borrow from the United States during the war. So Britain ended the war owing money.

Even so, people felt it was good to have the war over and they looked forward to a peaceful future. **Winston Churchill** had been Prime Minister during the war and he had been a very good leader. He was leader of the **Conservative Party**.

The 1945 election

Churchill decided to call a general election. Because he had been so popular during the war, he expected the Conservative Party would be elected again. To his surprise, the Labour Party won. Labour got 180 seats more than the Conservatives.

Why did Labour win?

Although the Labour win was a surprise, there were good reasons for it.

1 The Conservatives had been in power in the 1930s which was not a good time. Many people were poor and hungry then. They were afraid that if they voted for the Conservatives again, they would go back to this way of life.

2 Labour said that they would create a 'new Britain' in which everyone would have jobs and houses. There would be well run factories and better systems for looking after people when they were sick or old. Many soldiers coming back from the *First World War* had become very poor. Their families did not want this to happen again.

3 The last general election had been in 1935. This meant that nobody under the age of 30 had ever voted before. Most of these new voters voted Labour.

Austerity

The new Prime Minister was **Clement Attlee**. He felt that, as Britain had defeated the wartime enemy, Hitler, then poverty, the peace time enemy, could be defeated also.

After the war Britain had hardly any money and had to borrow millions of pounds. It was necessary to try to sell more to other countries and not to buy so much from abroad. Nearly all the cars made in Britain were exported. This meant that it was nearly impossible to buy a car in Britain and second hand cars were dearer than new ones!

In 1947 there was a very cold winter, but there was very little coal. There were power cuts and some factories had to close. There was a world shortage of food so food was still rationed after the war. This period of doing without was known as **austerity**.

Housing

There had been many poor slums before the war which needed to be replaced. Also many homes had been destroyed in the wartime bombing. The Labour government built thousands of houses between 1947 and 1950. There were ways in which houses could be built quickly, easily and cheaply. The 'Pre-fab' and the 'Orlit' were two common types built at this time. You can still see many of these houses today.

Nationalisation

Labour believed that industry and transport should be run by the state and not by private owners. When the state takes over a company, it is known as **nationalisation**. Labour nationalised many industries such as iron and steel, coalmines and London Transport.

As well as all these changes the new government introduced the **welfare state**.

Post-War housing: The proud occupants of a new 'Orlit' style bungalow at Lisnaskea, Co Fermanagh.

?

1 Does the cartoon on page 50 make you think that it would be good to vote for the Labour party? Why?

2 Imagine you are living at the end of 1947. Write about how you feel now that the war is over, and about what life is like now.

3 Why do you think so many things were scarce after the war?

4 Find out about Orlits. Describe one.

A working class street in Belfast shortly after the Second World War.

Today we take free health care almost for granted, but before 1948, things were very different. If you were sick, you had to pay the doctor to come and see you. If you needed medicine, you had to pay the full cost of it. If you needed to go into hospital, you had to pay for that too.

Rich people could pay for medical bills, but for most people, becoming ill could mean death because they could not afford to get treatment.

The Beveridge Report 1942

People felt that if the government could spend millions of pounds fighting Germany, it could also spend money on helping the sick. In 1942, **Sir William Beveridge** wrote a report in which he said there should be a system of state health care. Everybody would have to pay a charge, called **national insurance**, which would pay for this new scheme. Ordinary people thought this was a great idea, but there was disagreement in the government. Some said it wouldn't work and others said it would be too expensive.

The 1945 Labour Government

When Labour won the election in 1945, they promised to carry out what the Beveridge Report suggested. **Aneuran Bevan** was appointed Minister of Health. Getting everything ready was an enormous job but eventually the **Appointed Day** came, **5 July 1948**, and the **National Health Service** came into being. This was a very important thing which had happened in the lives of ordinary people. To explain what was happening, the government printed thousands of leaflets.

Also, every single person in the country had to have medical records. Remember that there were no computers then. Everything had to be written on paper. These paper records were known as 'hard copy'. The headquarters were at Newcastle on Tyne in England, and they took up 64 acres! There were 100 huge rooms holding a total of 25 million files. There were 1000 offices around the country and 17,000 staff were employed to look after it all.

STACKED ON THE COUNTER WERE SPECTACLES, WITH A LARGE CARD WITH A LARGE *A* GOING DOWN TO A SMALL *Z*.... I CAN SEE MY FATHER NOW, TRYING ON DIFFERENT PAIRS OF GLASSES, LOOKING AT THE CARD, PUTTING DOWN A PAIR, PICKING ANOTHER PAIR UP, UNTIL HE GOT THE SELECTED PAIR.... I'D SAY 'YOU LOOK SMASHING, DAD, 'AND THEN WE'D JUST GO OUT OF THE STORE.

Mr Law, quoted in **Now the War is Over** by Paul Addison, 1985.

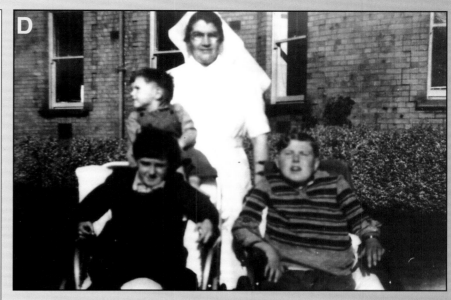

D

Polio was a major problem in the post-war years, and the new National Health Service did much to tackle it. Here are three victims at Belvoir Park Hospital, Belfast, in 1951. One of them is the author. Guess which!

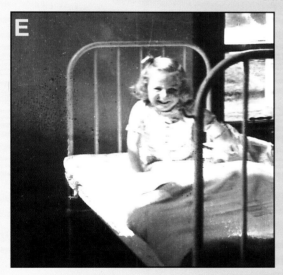

E

A young Tuberculosis (TB) patient at Greenisland Hospital in 1948.

Opposition to the National Health Service

At first, doctors were afraid that they wouldn't be working for themselves any more, but could be told what to do by the government. Most of them changed their minds when Bevan agreed that they could take private patients (who would still pay to be treated) as well as National Health Service patients.

The Appointed Day

The National Health Service began on 5th July 1948. Many people who were sick just before this didn't go for treatment until this date because then they would be treated free. Not just doctors, but also dentists and opticians were free. In the first few months millions of prescriptions were given out.

Developments after 1948

The new health service helped many people, but there were problems in the first few years. Hospitals were old, and there were not enough beds for all the people who could now be treated free.

It also cost millions of pounds more than the government though that it would.

?

1 What was meant by the 'Appointed Day'?

2 List as many reasons as you can why the early National Health service cost so much.

3 Read Source C. Do you think this took place *before* or *after* the Appointed Day? Why do you think so?

College Square, Belfast, in 1953. Only eight years after the war ended this street scene is dominated by cars that are still largely pre-war in design. Note also the UTA half-cab buses and the pony and trap. The street is cobbled and tram lines are in evidence. The statue of Rev Henry Cooke is known as 'The Black Man'.

Northern Ireland in 1945

Life was very difficult in Northern Ireland when the war ended. Because of the Blitz of 1941, large parts of Belfast had no houses, shops or factories. There were shortages of many items and factories and machinery were in bad need of repairs and renewals.

The Housing Problem

Housing was the worst problem. Not nearly as many houses had been built in Northern Ireland as had been built in the rest of the United Kingdom. Those which had been built were mostly for better off people and not for the poor. Many people still lived in houses without inside toilets or running water.

In 1944, an enquiry into the housing situation in Northern Ireland found that thousands of new houses were needed. In fact, 43,000 houses were unfit for living in.

The solution was for local councils to build more good houses for renting but, in Northern Ireland, politics influenced who got a house and where they got it. Many councillors got houses for people they knew. Because at this time most councillors were Unionist, Catholics sometimes didn't get a good house. If you were a Protestant who didn't know a councillor, it could be hard for you to get a house too.

Another organisation which built houses for rent was the **Northern Ireland Housing Trust**, set up by the Government in 1945. It used central government money and did not depend on local government. Woodlands Estate in Gilford,

Co Down, is a good example of a Housing Trust estate.

The Housing Trust used a points system for allocating houses, so it didn't matter who you knew, but they did give houses to families which were 'respectable'. This meant that the very poor were not likely to be given a Housing Trust home.

The Labour Government

When Labour won the election in 1945, the Unionists were worried. Labour was usually sympathetic to nationalism, and Unionists feared that the subject of a united Ireland might come up.

But Labour appreciated all Northern Ireland had done in the war, and how important it had been to Britain. So, in fact, when Labour was elected, Northern Ireland entered a very good period.

The Welfare State

Over the next fifteen years, people's health got much better. The number of cases of polio and TB went down. Instead of having the worst death rate in the United Kingdom, by 1962 it had the lowest!

Education

Another reform was the **1947 Education Act**. This said that all children should go on to free secondary education at the age of eleven. This Act also gave Catholic schools more money. Because of the Education Act, many new schools had to be built. It took years to build them all, but many of the high schools and secondary schools you see today were built at this time.

Another early post-war scene, this time at Donegall Square North with the City Hall visible on the right. Note the two way traffic where it is now one way and the trolley bus turning out of Donegal Place.

Housing Trust estate at Woodlands, Gilford, Co Down in the 1950s.

?

1 Look at the pictures A and B. Talk or write about what you see in them and what would be different today.

2 Look at the children in the picture on page 52 and in picture C above. Which ones were likely to be healthier?

3 How did life in the North get better between 1945 and 1949? Did it get better for all?

3.4 THE ÉIRE ECONOMY, 1945-49

After 1937, the Irish Free State was also called Éire. Even though Éire had not taken part in the Second World War, it was very much affected by it. Coal and other materials had been very scarce during the war, because Britain could not afford to send much to Éire. Britain needed all its own resources for itself. After the war Britain still needed most of its own resources to help rebuild its own economy.

Austerity

So, even though it had been neutral, Éire found it hard to get over the war. There was a depression, prices went up and many people had no work. Many people emigrated. Very few new houses were built.

The weather was wet in the summer of 1946 and the following winter. This meant that the crops of wheat were very poor and bread had to be rationed. In January 1947, de Valera announced that the country was still in a state of emergency. He said that things could get even more difficult.

O'Connell Street, Dublin in 1949: Carts, bicycles, trams, buses and the typical black painted cars of this period.

Coal shortages

Because Éire had almost no coal of its own, it depended on getting supplies from Britain. In 1945, Britain's coal-mining industry was in a poor state. The bad winter of 1947 meant that people needed a lot of coal for heating. Trains needed coal but there wasn't enough to go round. Some trains were changed so that they could run on oil.

The 1948 election

People were having a hard time in Éire and they were not very happy about it. They were even more unhappy when reports came back from Britain and the North about the benefits of the Welfare State and the new Health Service. Because of unhappiness with the government, new political parties were formed. The main one was **Clann na Poblachta**. This was set up in 1946 by **Sean McBride**.

Train converted to oil burning in 1948.

Sean McBride, leader of Clann na Poblachta.

There was an election in 1948. De Valera's party lost, and he lost power for the first time since 1932. A new Inter-Party government was formed, made up of several different parties. It was led by **John Costello**, who was the leader of the **Fine Gael** party.

The Inter-Party Government 1948 to 1951

From 1948 on, the Irish economy began to change. Up to now, the government had tried to spend as little as possible, and make people earn enough money to build up their own farms and businesses. The new government decided to give money to help new industry and business and to encourage exports to other countries. Two new organisations were set up:

1 The **Industrial Development Authority** (IDA). This organisation gave grants of money to industries and also gave them advice if they had any problems.
2 **The Export Board**. This organisation tried to increase sales of Irish goods to the USA and Canada.

These two new bodies were very successful and by 1953 Irish industry had improved greatly compared to 1946. Éire and Britain started to get on a bit better at this time. In 1948, a new trade agreement meant that Irish farmers got a better price for their produce, specially cattle.

In spite of this, in 1949 the Irish economy was not doing as well as the British one and thousands of people were emigrating from Ireland every year.

?

1 Do you think the Éire government was to blame for *all* its difficulties just after the war?

2 Compare life in Northern Ireland (Unit 3.3) with life in Éire (Unit 3.4) just after the war. In what ways was it the same and in what ways was it different? Think about topics like housing, austerity, health care, industry.

As we saw on page 49, Britain and Éire had disagreed deeply about the events of the Second World War. Churchill had been particularly annoyed that Éire had stayed neutral.

De Valera 1945-1948

Just after the war, Ireland was rather friendless. It wasn't on good terms with either Britain or the United States. This meant that its economy couldn't recover very quickly because these other countries were not in a mood to help.

The Republic declared 1949

Officially, Éire was still part of the British Commonwealth, but it had removed all mention of the King of England from its

---

WHAT DO WE CALL THE SOUTH?

Irish Free State — This was the name used from 1922 until 1949, when Ireland became a republic. Many people, including some northern Nationalists, continued to use it after 1949. The Irish for Free State is Saorstát Éireann. This appeared on coins until 1937, when the word Éire began to be used.

Republic of Ireland — This term was used to refer to the South after it became a republic in 1949. It often appears on letters from the UK to the South to avoid confusion with Northern Ireland. Northern Unionists also use this title, though it is unpopular south of the border, where the preferred form of address is Ireland if the rest of the address is in English and Éire if it is in Irish. Sometimes the term used is Irish Republic.

Éire — This is Irish for Ireland, the name adopted for the South in the 1937 Constitution. It was used on stamps from 1922 and from 1937 onwards it appeared on coins. This name has been used throughout this book to refer to the South after 1937, because it appears on a lot of official documents of this period, and was commonly used by contemporaries referring to the South. The title Ireland can lead to confusion as it also refers to the *island* of Ireland (which includes the North).

---

constitution. Really, Éire *was* a republic, although it wasn't called this. The new Inter-Party government of 1948 wanted to sort this out once and for all.

Clann na Poblachta also wanted to start putting pressure on Britain again to end partition. Now that the war was over, people were able to start thinking about the border again.

Éire left the Commonwealth, a special Act was passed in the Dáil called the **Republic of Ireland Act 1948**, and Éire became the **Republic of Ireland** on **Easter Monday 1949**, exactly 33 years after the Easter Rising of 1916.

Northern Ireland and the Republic

In the North, there were different points of view about this declaration. Unionists saw it as a threat, specially when there was talk once more of trying to end partition.

Many northern Nationalists were not happy that the South was calling itself the *Irish* Republic, because it was only 26 of the counties of Ireland. They continued to call it the *Irish Free State*, and thought that the name *Irish Republic* or *Republic of Ireland* should only be used when there was a 32 county republic.

Britain and the Republic

It was expected that the British government would be very unhappy with Éire's decision to declare a republic and leave the British Commonwealth, but in fact, Britain's reaction was very calm.

Britain passed the **Ireland Act, 1949**. This recognised the Republic and made special mention of the position of Northern Ireland as part of the United Kingdom. The two most important points of the Ireland Act were:

1 Irish citizens would still be treated as though they *were* British subjects when they were in Britain, even though they were no longer British. This meant that you did not need a passport to get into Britain, or a work permit to work there. Irish people could also vote in British elections. The same conditions applied to British people in the Republic.

2 Britain would continue to give better trading terms to the Republic of Ireland than it did to other countries in Europe. So the Republic still had some of the benefits of being in the Commonwealth without actually being a member.

The Partition issue

Partition continued to be a sore point between the Republic and Britain. When the Republic left the Commonwealth, Unionists felt that they would like a united Ireland even less. Partition was going to end only if reuniting with the South seemed to be a good idea to the Unionists. Éire leaving the Commonwealth in 1949 only made Unionists glad that Northern Ireland was separate from it.

Éire and NATO

Éire also refused to join the **North Atlantic Treaty Organisation** which was set up in 1949. The Southern government said that, because of partition, it couldn't join Britain in a military alliance.

?

1 Why do you think Éire wanted to leave the British Commonwealth?

2 How would each of the following have felt about the declaration of the Irish Republic in 1949: (a) a member of Clann na Poblachta, (b) a northern Unionist, (c) a northern Nationalist?

3 When Éire left the British Commonwealth it made it even *less* likely that partition would end. Why?

Northern Ireland enjoyed a very good relationship with Britain just after the war and for a long time afterwards. One of the reasons for this was the way that Northern Ireland had helped Britain in the war.

Labour and Northern Ireland

In the past, the British Labour Party had been favourable to Irish Nationalists. When Labour came to power in 1945 the Ulster Unionists were rather worried.

Nationalist MPs took their seats in Stormont and some northern Nationalists set up the **Anti-Partition League** in 1945.

Attlee was the British Prime Minister and he watched the Unionist government in Northern Ireland to see how it was treating the Catholic minority. Attlee was specially keen that everybody benefited equally from the new Welfare State.

However, Labour knew that the British public were sympathetic to Northern Ireland at this time and they did not push for a united Ireland.

WHAT DO WE CALL THE NORTH?

Northern Ireland — This is the official name for the North according to the Government of Ireland Act, 1920 which also called the South Southern Ireland. It is the preferred name among Unionists and in the UK. Many Nationalists dislike this name, partly because it is seen as recognising the legitimacy of partition and partly because Co Donegal is further north than parts of Northern Ireland!

Ulster — This name is commonly used in everyday conversation, by people who really mean Northern Ireland. It is not strictly correct as Ulster includes Donegal, Cavan and Monaghan which are not part of Northern Ireland. Many people in the North like the term because it gives them a regional identity (eg Ulster Fry and Ulsterbus).

The Six Counties — This name is often used by those who do not want to refer to the North as either Ulster or Northern Ireland. It is the name most commonly used by Southern politicians, and is also common among Northern Nationalists.

SIR BASIL : "DEV COULDN'T CRACK IT, SO YOU'D BETTER GIVE UP THE BIG IDEA."

(Hugh McAteer was the leader of the IRA in the 1940s.)

SOURCE *'The Voice of Ulster', March 1948.*

The 1949 Stormont election

When Éire left the Commonwealth and declared a republic in 1949, Unionists were alarmed. The new government in the South called for an end to partition and asked Unionists to agree. **Sir Basil Brooke** was the Prime Minister of Northern Ireland and he said at this time "Ulster is not for sale".

In 1949, Brooke decided to call an election and ask the people of Northern Ireland to vote on the Union. The Ulster Unionist party won by a big majority. This election divided people in Northern Ireland and led to such bad feeling that there was some street rioting.

The Ireland Act 1949

This Act recognised the Republic of Ireland, but it also stated very clearly that Northern Ireland was part of the United Kingdom (see Source C).

This reassured Unionists that, even though Éire said it should rule the North, there could be no change to Northern Ireland without the consent of its own parliament at Stormont.

The Baby Sitter (Dublin Opinion)

The Welfare State

Labour was keen to bring the social services in Northern Ireland up to the standards of the rest of the United Kingdom. To do this, Britain had to spend a lot of money on Northern Ireland from this time on. Northern Ireland was also taxed in the same way as the rest of Britain.

Northern Ireland was very prosperous for the next twenty years or so. However, some people felt that political changes and reforms were necessary. The Civil Rights Campaign began in the late 1960s and this started a new chapter in the history of Northern Ireland.

PARLIAMENT HEREBY DECLARES THAT NORTHERN IRELAND REMAINS PART OF HIS MAJESTY'S DOMINIONS AND OF THE UNITED KINGDOM AND AFFIRMS THAT IN NO EVENT WILL NORTHERN IRELAND OR ANY PART THEREOF CEASE TO BE A PART OF HIS MAJESTY'S DOMINIONS AND OF THE UNITED KINGDOM WITHOUT THE CONSENT OF THE PARLIAMENT OF NORTHERN IRELAND.
Ireland Act, June 1949, Clause 1 (1) B

?

1 When the Ireland Act was passed what do you think (a) a northern Unionist and (b) southern Nationalist would have thought about it?

2 Explain the point that Cartoon A is making. What do you think Cartoon B is about? The people are Britannia, John Bull and Brooke. The baby represents the Nationalist minority.

1933-38		**Anglo-Irish trade war**
1935		Stanley Baldwin Prime Minister
		Britain begins to rearm
1935-6		Italy invades Ethiopia
1936		Edward VIII king
		Abdication crisis
		George VI king
	Nov	Rome-Berlin Axis
1936-39		Spanish Civil War
1937		Neville Chamberlain Prime Minister
		New constitution for Éire
1938	Jan	General election in Northern Ireland
	March	Anschluss between Germany and Austria
	Sept-Oct	**Treaty Ports returned to Éire**
	Sept	Munich crisis
1939	Jan	IRA begin a bombing campaign in Britain
	March	Germany occupies Czechoslovakia
	April	Conscription introduced in Britain
	Aug	Nazi-Soviet Pact
	1 Sept	Germany invades Poland
	3 Sept	**Britain declares war on Germany**
	Sept	Children evacuated from British cities
	Dec	IRA raid on magazine fort in Phoenix Park, Dublin

1940	9 April	Germany invades Denmark and Norway
	9 May	**Winston Churchill made Prime Minister**
	10 May	Germany attacks Holland, Belgium and France
	4 June	Dunkirk evacuation completed
	22 June	**Surrender of France**
	July-Aug	**Battle of Britain**
	7 Sept	First German air raid on London
	14 Nov	Germans bomb Coventry
	Nov	**J M Andrews made Prime Minister of Northern Ireland**
1941	Feb	Castle Archdale flying boat base opened
	April-May	**Germans bomb Belfast**
	May	Sinking of the *Bismarck*
		Germans bomb North Strand in Dublin
	Dec	USA enters the war
1942	Jan	First US troops arrive in Northern Ireland
		Beveridge Report
1943		**Sir Basil Brooke becomes Prime Minister of Northern Ireland**
1944	6 June	D-Day landings in france
1945	2 May	De Valera sympathises over the death of Hitler
	7 May	**German surrender**
	8 May	VE Day
	11 May	Churchill's speech attacking Éire's neutrality
	16 May	De Valera's reply

1945 **July British general election. Attlee Prime Minister**

2 Sept Japanese surrender

1946 Bread rationing introduced in the UK

Formation of Clann na Poblachta

1947 Jan Severe weather hits Britain

Coal industry, and electricity nationalised in Britain

Education Act (N Ireland)

1948 Jan British railways are nationalised

Feb General election in Éire

Inter-party government formed. John Costello becomes taoiseach

Anglo-Irish trade agreement

5 July Appointed Day for the start of the **National health Service**

Republic of Ireland Act passed

1949 Feb Northern Ireland general election

April Irish Republic declared

Ireland Act passed (Westminster)